The Girl in the Back Seat

My Walk with God through Domestic Violence

TRACI SILVA

CLAY BRIDGES
PRESS

The Girl in the Back Seat
My Walk with God through Domestic Violence

ISBN 978-1-953300-37-9 (paperback)
ISBN 978-1-953300-38-6 (ebook)

Special Sales: Most Clay Bridges titles are available in special quantity discounts. Custom imprinting or excerpting can also be done to fit special needs. For standard bulk orders, go to www.claybridgesbulk.com. For specialty press or large orders, contact Clay Bridges at info@claybridgespress.com.

*To honor the L*ORD

For my family

Thank you . . .

Mike, for everything you are.
Janet Pippin, for your support, critique, and encouragement.
Sherri Taylor, for your eye for detail and your laugh.

When my father and my mother forsake me,
Then the Lord *will take care of me.*

—Ps. 27:10 NKJV

It is not the critic who counts; not the man who points out how the strong man stumbles, or where the doer of deeds could have done better. The credit belongs to the man who is actually in the arena, whose face is marred by dust and sweat and blood; who strives valiantly; who errs, who comes short again and again, because there is no effort without error and shortcoming; but who does actually strive to do the deeds; who knows great enthusiasms, the great devotions; who spends himself in a worthy cause; who at the best knows in the end the triumph of high achievement, and who at the worst, if he fails, at least fails while daring greatly, so that his place shall never be with those cold and timid souls who neither know victory nor defeat.

—Theodore Roosevelt

Success is not final, failure is not fatal: it is the courage to continue that counts.

—Winston Churchill

Have enough courage to trust love one more time and always one more time.

—Maya Angelou

God Only Knows

Wide awake while the world is sound asleepin'
Too afraid of what might show up while you're
dreamin'
Nobody, nobody, nobody sees you
Nobody, nobody would believe you
Every day you try to pick up all the pieces
All the memories, they somehow never leave you
Nobody, nobody, nobody sees you
Nobody, nobody would believe you

. . .

You keep a cover over every single secret
So afraid if someone saw them they would leave
Somebody, somebody, somebody sees you
Somebody, somebody will never leave you
God only knows what you've been through
God only knows what they say about you
God only knows how it's killing you
But there's a kind of love that God only knows

. . .

For the lonely, for the ashamed
The misunderstood, and the ones to blame
What if we could start over
We could start over
We could start over
'Cause there's a kind of love that God only knows

—*"God Only Knows," for King & Country*

Contents

Introduction

It wasn't talked about—what went on in our house. Silence was learned and became a good friend. There's a place on the wall in my bedroom that I stared at as a kid while I listened to screaming and fighting, the echoes of war being played out under our roof. Mom would sob as Dad demeaned her, tore her down, and interrogated her.

Staring at the spot, I could block out the fresh cuts and bruises Mom wore. The place on the wall was the black hole to anywhere I wanted to go. "Calgon, take me away." Drifting off, I could make the battle like background noise.

The choices my parents made affected me, but I didn't know it. That discovery happened when I found myself making the same choices and landing in similar piles of crap, and then I blamed my parents.

I was mad that Mom wasn't stronger. Her mental health created a lot of confusion for me, especially about communicating with God.

I was angry that Dad was an alcoholic. He served in World War II and then brought it home and served it to his family. My fear of Dad caused me to be petrified of the Lord.

My brothers and I went through it all together. Because of them, I related to Jesus as my Brother and accepted Him as my Savior at age 15. But I fell out of the church within a year.

It took me until age 28 to realize that women aren't subservient punching bags to be demeaned and devalued. It has taken just as long for it to really sink in that I am a child of God.

Without realizing the value of what I learned in church, I hung onto what I was taught. In hindsight, I know God hung onto me and saved my life many times—through excruciating loneliness, physical and emotional abuse, thoughts of suicide, and rape. It would get bad, but the Lord was always there providing a way out, a choice.

* * *

Webster's Dictionary defines domestic violence[1] as "violent or abusive behavior directed by one family or household member against another."

From experience, I can vouch that being raised in intimidation with parents threatening to leave each other, threats of financial cut-off, physical and sexual abuse, verbal assaults, and psychological games affects kids over time. Eventually, somewhere down the road and well into adulthood, those children are left feeling isolated and lost, trying to put pieces back together that never fit in the first place.

It's torture.

The mind games and tit-for-tat kids see between parents are more often than not what they will model later in life, even when they are determined not to. Violence is a display of power that God uses to correct. We use it to destroy. It's the opposite of the relationship, love, and peace He created us for.[2]

> *Even if it was written in Scripture long ago, you can be sure it's written for us. God wants the combination of his steady, constant calling and warm, personal counsel in Scripture to come to characterize us, keeping us alert for whatever he will do next. May our dependably steady and warmly personal God*

*develop maturity in you so that you get along with
each other as well as Jesus gets along with us all.*[3]

The Apostle Paul is telling us that things written in the Bible were written for our learning and salvation. In our human uncertainty, studying ancient times and the bravery of the saints helps us make better choices going forward as individuals and as a nation. Instead of following in their footsteps, we learn from their mistakes. If we want to make changes in the world today, we have to look back. Similarly, in our upbringing, we learn from our parents. We also learn from their mistakes.

With spiritual eyes open wide, wonder sometimes creeps in. What would it have been like if different choices had been made?

God knows everything we're going to go through because of sin.[4]

What a ripple effect. Adam was told to protect the Garden of Eden and not eat of one particular tree. Then one tempting conversation and one piece of fruit, and history has repeated itself over and over. Sin has snowballed into what we have today. The phrase "history repeats itself" takes on a very literal meaning when we dive into the Bible.

* * *

The Word tells us about abuses to women. In ancient times, rape and assaults on women weren't covered up or ignored. They were addressed and avenged. These crimes caused cultural outrage and more violence, and a few sparked civil wars.

Genesis tells us about Jacob's daughter, Dinah, who was violated by Shechem. So her brothers murdered him and many more in revenge.[5]

Judges tells us about the unnamed concubine who was gang-raped and left for dead by men of the tribe of Benjamin. Other tribes went to war against them for the injustice done to her.[6]

Second Samuel tells of Tamar who was raped by her half-brother Amnon. Then her brother Absalom killed him. It sparked rebellion against Absalom's father, King David, who would be in the bloodline of Jesus.[7]

God never intended for women to be violated. He intended for all to be protected and valued.[8] The Lord protects and provides for the vulnerable. God is our justice. "Do not take revenge, my dear friends, but leave room for God's wrath, for it is written: "'It is mine to avenge; I will repay,' says the Lord.'"[9]

* * *

While domestic violence is about power, it's a choice made in pride—ego that believes it can dominate and subdue, control and manipulate. Looking into the eyes and face of an offender is the closest thing you can get to seeing the nature of Satan. We have introduced our kids to that choice and the stigma it brings.

It's like a disease that breeds some of the worst in society. One in 15 children is exposed to intimate partner violence each year, and 90 percent of those children are eyewitnesses to the violence.[10]

We watch other nations grow hate and are appalled at things their children are exposed to, but we barely look in our own backyards.

There are better laws and protections now, but domestic violence remains uncomfortable, not understood, and shameful. It's everything dark and satanic. People don't want to talk about it or hear about it. But it goes on, breeding hostility, anger, resentment, and hate.

There are many more consequences of domestic violence— PTSD, mental health, depression, anxiety, thoughts of suicide—to name a few.

* * *

When I first put my fingertips to a computer keyboard for what I viewed as an unwanted venture, the only path I saw the Lord taking me on was the destructive memory lane that is my past—a past I had shoved down into the pit of my own personal hell. But the resurgence of life and hope brought to light by following His guidance is why I am sharing this as my testimony to the amazing love and greatness of our Lord.

I pray my walk with God opens hearts and minds to Jesus and what He did for us, and to the Spirit who is within each and every one of us if we will just turn to Jesus and tap into Him. It's not about religion or law, ceremony or custom. It's realizing who we are and why we were created. It's knowing that what we go through here on earth is for a reason.

We have one life. It's eternal. What we believe determines how we live in the hereafter once we die. We all go through it. We're not here to go it alone, but we have to make the choice.

We're all children of the great I AM. Just realize it!

1

By age five, my survival skills were being honed through violence, intimidation, and fear. Knowing how to stay hidden was already ingrained in me. Alcoholism, disrespect, screaming, yelling, and mental illness were life. Rejection and agonizing loneliness were my closest enemies.

* * *

When my younger brother, Todd, came along, I was five. Todd came home one day, but Mom didn't—not for a few months. She'd had a nervous breakdown after his birth and was institutionalized. That's what they called it, the people around me who whispered loud enough for me to hear. That's what neighbors and "friends" helping Dad take care of us kids said.

"What's the state ward?" I shyly asked Dad one evening.

"It's a psychiatric hospital." He gave me a scrunched-up hum face as if to say, "Where'd you hear that?" Then he added, "Your mom's getting some help because she wasn't feeling well. Would you like to see her?"

"Can I?"

"Yes. I know she'd like to see you."

* * *

Dad took me and my older brother, Tom, to see Mom.

The repugnant musty air of sickness and cleanser is what hit me first. The next sensory outburst came from a scream somewhere off in the distance. It was loud and faded out in agony. Tom and I grabbed each other's hands and looked at each other with that side eye that says, "I got you."

Dad checked us in, and then we were led into an open cafeteria-style room with several round tables that could fit about six people each.

"Paula will be right out," the nurse told Dad. "You kids have a great visit with your mom," she nodded to us and walked off.

I surveyed the room as we waited. Some other people were sitting at two of the tables. At a glance, it was clear we had something in common by the mixed look of disbelief and confusion on all our faces. Scanning the room further, I saw shelves full of games, puzzles, and books; a couple vending machines; and a door leading to the bathroom.

*

I caught sight of Mom as soon as the doors opened and froze in fear. She resembled the woman I knew but in zombie form—blotchy red face and long greasy hair tied back in a bun. As she shuffled across the room, her slippers softly grazing the floor, a nurse held one of her arms, steadying her. Mom's head bobbed slightly with the motion of her body, and her robe hung loosely over pale blue pajamas.

She approached with a blank, faraway look in her eyes, and I didn't know if she recognized me. Then she said, "Hi, Honey" in a weird sort of drawl.

Warming up to her slowly but cautiously, we sat down at a table to visit. Extremely medicated, she was spaced out.

The nurse brought some items to the table, and Mom reached for something. Her arm worked slowly as she lifted it up from her lap. Her eyes, head, and upper body followed her hand as it moved over the table like a mechanical crane. She showed me and Tom the crafts she'd been working on as Dad stepped to the background to allow us to visit.

"Here, Honey, I made you something."

Mom didn't sound like herself, her voice crackling like Miss Gulch's.[1] She pushed two pieces over to me. One was smaller and slid the closest to me.

"It's a ring, Honey, made out of a dollar bill."

That is what it was, folded tightly, origami style, with the "1" almost perfectly in the center, raised up just a bit to resemble the stone of a ring.

"It's pretty cool. You folded it like this?"

"Yes," she slurred. "They taught me that here. Look at the other one."

It was a Native American style necklace with brown and white beads and a yellow and red butterfly in the square pendant. From the bottom hung a tri-colored beaded fringe of orange, red, and yellow.

"It's pretty. You made this, too?"

"Yes. It's a necklace. Like the Indians make, Honey."

"It looks just like what they make, Mom. Thank you."

She was so proud, the kind of pride I had when I brought her handmade crafts from school. She seemed childlike and simple, not Mom, and it gave me an eerie feeling. I chose to never see her in the hospital again.

* * *

When I was growing up, Mom was always around but rarely present. Her mental health issues made her frail, mentally and physically. It was like walking on eggshells in our house. Tom and I were usually on edge, keeping an eye out for Todd and watching out for Mom while trying not to do or say anything that might tip her over the edge. We also waited for the other shoe to drop when Dad got home.

Mom never spoke of her illness or the abuse she endured. The silence and quiet suffering Mom displayed confused me when it came to speaking up for myself, communication in personal relationships, and socializing.

Her example became my understanding of how I should behave and be treated.

*

Mom is a mix of German and English, raised in Willoughby, Ohio, a city rich in the culture of the Erie Indians who first resided in the area. The city developed a thriving tourist trade and attracted business from nearby Cleveland.[2]

She was raised by two terrific people. Grandpa worked for the railroad, and Grandma headed the cafeteria for the local elementary school. Mom grew up with her only sister, Jan. Although my grandparents were wonderful people, their relationship was ugly. They argued constantly, called each other names, and screamed and yelled at one another.

Card games were the worst.

"Oh, Paul," Grandma would hiss from across the table. "You can't play that. You're such an ass."

"Keep to yourself, woman," Grandpa would shoot back. "Shut up and let me play my way."

You'd have thought they were archenemies the way they snarled at each other. If the game made it to the end, they'd be so pissed off at one another that they'd have to stay away from each other. Those were my favorite times—spending time with one without the other around.

Grandpa would storm off. He liked to drive, and he'd either go on a ride by himself or take us kids with him. Even though he'd be steaming at Grandma, he never took it out on us and never drove like he was mad. It was always on Grandpa's time, which was slow. That was also a bone of contention with Grandma.

He'd take us to Daniel Park where we'd go fishing or just walk along the creek skipping stones or trying to catch crawdads. Grandpa was always talkative without Grandma around, and he loved to tell stories.

Grandma was the same way without Grandpa around.

Aunt Jan and Mom seemed to have a good relationship. Our families visited often when I was young, but something happened over the course of time, and they didn't speak for more than 30 years. Even when Grandma passed away, Mom and Jan could barely stand to be in the same room together.

* * *

It wasn't until I was in my 50s that I finally dared to ask Mom questions. It was during a time that I was trying to untwist and release emotions that I had only a superficial understanding of, things needing to be untangled in my own life.

"How did you and Dad meet?"

"He worked next to the salon where I worked. He was a goofball, and I enjoyed that he was a funny guy."

"Mom, why didn't you ever call the police or ask for help?"

"Sometimes, I fought back or tried to defend myself. Your dad would have scratches or bruises on him, too, and he'd threaten to take you kids away." And she sobbed.

"Why didn't any family ever step in? I think they knew what was going on."

"Oh, they were very aware of the hell we were living in. I don't know why. Guess it was easier to turn their heads."

"Grandma was the only one who ever said anything to me about our home life. She told me she prayed for us."

"Grandma knew the situation," Mom said sadly. "It was awful. I don't know why your dad beat me so bad." It came out in a whimper.

"When we lived on Cedarbrook, you always had bruises."

"He'd come home drunk and be in a state. When I wasn't interested in him sexually, he'd force himself on me."

"How often did he hit you, Mom?"

"Oh . . ." she paused as if not wanting to go down memory lane. "It happened every two to three weeks. But every night, it was always something. He'd find fault with anything. I dreaded him coming home."

"When you'd get sick, what would happen?"

"Oh, it started as depression after you were born. It was postpartum depression."

*

Grandma told me once that Mom's problems started after I was born. When I got older and was out of the house, I asked Dad about it.

"What's wrong with Mom? What's her diagnosis?"

"When we brought you home after you were born, I got a call at work one day from our landlord. He told me someone found your mom walking around the apartment complex naked, with you in her arms, and she was babbling nonsense. She landed in the hospital for the first time and was diagnosed as bipolar and schizophrenic."

*

Mom's illness came in cycles, usually twice a year. Tom and I learned to recognize when her health started to fade. She'd lose interest in taking care of herself. Her skin and hair would get oily, and her face would break out in a rashy type of acne. After a couple of weeks, her speech would become erratic. She'd begin to talk nonsensically, and eventually she'd be gone completely, vanishing into some other space and time and talking to people and things we had no knowledge of.

* * *

The alcoholism and violence in Dad versus the good in him was a huge reason for my confusion when it came to personal relationships and socializing. Dad was Serbian, raised in Salem in eastern rural Ohio. The city was founded by Quakers who were known for aiding in the abolishment of slavery. The area was plush with trees—big oaks that dropped acorns everywhere, box elder trees with creepy black and red bugs, and maple trees that produced some of the world's best syrup. Fall in Ohio was spectacular with a display of color in preparation for winter hibernation.

My grandparents were immigrants:

> In 1900, fewer than ten thousand Serbian immigrants resided in Ohio. By 1920, more than thirty thousand Yugoslavians resided in Ohio. Serbia was part of Yugoslavia at this time. Most of these Yugoslavians and Serbians settled along Lake Erie, especially in Cleveland, where they found low-paying jobs in factories or as day laborers. In 1914, approximately one thousand Serbs resided in Cleveland alone. More successful immigrants established businesses that supplied their fellow migrants with traditional Serbian products. In Cleveland, the Serbian immigrants tended to settle in their own communities or with other Southern Europeans, including Slovenes and Croatians, preferring to live among people who shared similar cultural beliefs and spoke the same language as they did. By the mid-1900s, Cleveland claimed at least two Serbian communities. Most Serbian immigrants were followers of the Orthodox Church. In Cleveland, by 1920, Serbians had also formed several social and cultural institutions, including St. Sava Lodge. Although they now resided in the United States, Serbians continued to practice many traditional customs and beliefs.[3]

Dad was proud of his heritage and could speak the language, although he seldom did so. He spoke of his family lovingly, except for his father whom he barely said a word about. He had eight brothers and sisters; a couple of them passed away in childhood.

The most he'd say about his family was during visits to the cemetery where many of Dad's immediate family rested. It's a beautiful old graveyard full of shade trees. My brothers and I would run around pelting each other with acorns until we got yelled at. We'd walk through the grounds, and Dad would point out headstones and talk about family members he'd lost. Some of the stones looked ancient and were written in Slavic.

One marker was for a small child, maybe three or four years old. Dad would grow somber.

"That's Anna," he said. "She pulled a vat of hot water over and was scalded to death. Back then, we washed clothes in a big, round vat, and she pulled it over. Her death almost killed majka [mother], but I was born right after."

He'd hold his arms out to describe the size of the washing vat and then pause while we stood there looking down at the small burial site.

Tom, Todd, and I would wait until Dad started walking away before we did because it was rare to see him vulnerable.

*

The next stop was Baba's [Grandma's] plot. Dad's mom passed away when I was six, and I barely remember her. But I can still envision her fluffy white cloud of hair and her little poodle named Omi. The smell of cabbage and sausage from her kitchen and the mouthwatering aroma of spices she concocted left their imprint on my senses.

"I miss her," Dad would say sadly. "She was an amazing woman."

He'd glance at his father's side of the headstone and then wave his hand in introduction. "That's Dedo [Grandpa]. He passed away when I was 17 while I was in the Navy."

The only other tidbit as to my elusive Dedo came from Aunt Mitza much later in life.

* * *

After Dad passed away in 2004, Todd and I were walking around the yard of Dad's childhood home with our aunt. She pointed out different areas and talked about playing as a kid. They were the same spots Dad used to talk about.

The picture of them running around the plush green lawn giggling and playing made me smile. The film reel in my mind could see them hiding behind trees and sneaking over to the old well that jutted up from the ground, trying to find each other in a game of hide and seek. Or maybe they went fishing at the pond across the way.

It was a great pond where my cousins, brothers, and I loved to play. It was swampy and dark from the big willows that had comingled their branches and formed an amazing tarp, giving shade to everything below and surrounding the pond.

Lying on the mossy ground, I'd stare up to watch the display of sun rays and color break through fleetingly here and there. It was nature's kaleidoscope.

"Aunt Mitza, what was Dad's relationship like with his dad?" I asked.

She hesitated a bit before answering, weighing her words.

"Dad used to pick on Stevie a lot because he was small."

"Pick on him? How?" Todd asked, trying for more information.

"You kids need to stop digging and move on," she snapped, ending the conversation.

Neither one of us understood what "move on" meant. She had never acknowledged that she knew about our home life.

It was typical of the communication from Dad's side of the family. Dad seemed like he wanted to be close with them but was more the "black sheep" of the family. His family wasn't welcoming, and it was uncomfortable when we visited.

* * *

Dad had two kids from a previous marriage—Steven and Karen. Steven passed away from leukemia at the age of eight. I met Karen at her wedding when I was five. It was also the first time I witnessed Dad drink. The wedding was at a golf course or some type of country club. Most of that day is a blur, confusing to me as a kid. It was extremely hurtful to see Dad so happy for a daughter who wasn't me—happy in a way that he'd rarely been around us.

Alcohol took over his body, and he morphed into someone else. Everything about him changed when he drank. He went from being happy-go-lucky to the meanest son-of-a. . . . He was a functioning alcoholic—an angry, mean drunk and an avid smoker.

Dad's first love was golf. When he wasn't at work, he was golfing, bowling, or socializing at bars. He worked hard to support us financially, but family was not his top priority.

* * *

The most interaction I had with Dad was either when I got hurt or in trouble. Mom wasn't good under pressure, so Dad was always called home whenever blood was involved. Another side of him, his loving and caring side, would kick in. It was the side I craved. He'd talk to me like he loved me.

I was riding behind Tom on his old Colt bicycle one day. As we rolled down Cedarbrook, he looked back at me and asked, "How you doing?"

"Fine," I smiled back.

Riding on a bike with the wind in my hair felt like freedom. Looking around at the neighborhood and then looking back behind us, everything went red. There was a trail of blood, and I cried out in fear as my eyes followed it to my ankle.

Tom looked back again, his eyes following the trail, and terror came over his face. He stopped the bike and carefully laid it and me down on the lawn next to where we stopped.

The lady in the house saw us and came running out with a towel. She gasped, went white, and then ran down and told Mom. Tom was terrified that he was going to get beat because he'd been told many times not to ride with anyone on his bike.

Someone untangled my foot, but when Dad showed up, he was my hero. He stayed with me and my mangled ankle the whole time. In the room next to us at the emergency room was a kid screaming bloody murder. When the doctor came in with a nurse to check on us, he thumbed toward the noise next door and said, "Sorry for all the commotion. Kid stuck his fingers in a metal blade fan."

Then the doctor spoke to me directly. "Let me take a look at this. How'd you do that?"

"On the back of her brother's bike," Dad said for me in that tone that says I was doing something I'd been told not to do. He looked at me because I had been warned just as many times as Tom.

"I didn't feel it happen until after," I meekly added.

"Well, you're a brave girl. Will you be okay for a few minutes while I go next door?"

"Yes."

"The bleeding is under control. Let's keep it iced. When I get back, we'll stitch it up," the doctor addressed the nurse.

After the doctor left, Dad pulled me close. "You're doing a lot better than the kid next door with his hurt fingers. I'm not going to scold you. I think you already got what's coming to you. Stay strong and brave. That's how you always have to be."

* * *

Dad's caring side would also show up for Mom when she got sick. It was extremely confusing how he could beat her like he did and then show the care for her that he did. It was a strange interaction to witness, as if he had no clue that he was the major contributing factor to her illness.

It was my understanding of love.

2

It was an exciting time when we moved to State College, Pennsylvania. Dad was eager to start his new job. He was into football and looked forward to seeing some college games. Mom was doing better and happy for the change. I hoped for a fresh start for our family.

* * *

With a gorgeous view of the Appalachian Mountains from our backyard, it was a constantly changing canvas of nature's beauty, a rotating wheel of color through the changing seasons. The smell of fall in the air was the best.

Nature was always an escape. As a kid, I'd often sit in the backyard or go for walks and find a place where no one else was around. With the still quiet of the world, I'd daydream and wonder how everything came to be.

Baba was the first person I knew who passed away, and it made me curious about where people went when they died. I didn't know what heaven was, but people told me that's where Baba went. I assumed it was in the sky somewhere because that's where people pointed when they talked about it.

Walks through the cemetery with Dad made me curious. Cartoons made me wonder about death. Where did people go when they went poof, like Jerry being chased by Tom.[1] Jerry would stop quickly and fold his hands. I knew that meant he was praying, but I didn't know what it meant.

*

Silence was a refuge for me, and in the quiet of nature was one of the most beautiful symphonies. The burble of a nearby brook kept tempo. Falling leaves through branches softly touched down with the tink of a triangle. The snare was lizards and other ground creepers flitting about on the dry ground making random crackles. Fingers of the breeze through the strings of the trees and their branches played harp and violin, while cicadas added varying tones of reeds. Included in the piece were the contrasting pitches of birds and other wildlife.

Although I was lonely, there was often a presence, something I didn't understand. It wasn't scary like situations at home; it was comforting. There was something pleasant in solitude, especially outdoors.

But no matter the change of scenery, there was no escaping the ugliness within the walls called home.

* * *

Dad now worked even later into the night and was rarely present for dinner. We kids were usually in bed by the time he showed up drunk and rank with the smell of booze and smoke. The fighting ensued almost nightly, but there were times when he just passed out.

It didn't take very long until Tom and I recognized Mom was getting sick again.

Mom had a habit of reading junk magazines and delving into them on her transition from the present to the unknown. The day she snapped, Dad was at work. Mom called me and Tom into the upstairs bathroom.

"Kids, listen. I have to keep you safe." The drawl was back. "These will keep you safe."

She turned to the sink and picked up the case that held her contact lenses. Tom and I gave each other the side eye, and we were on the ready.

"Tom, you're stronger, faster," she said. "Just don't look at them. I'll put these in Traci's eyes, and she'll be safe."

"What are you talking about?" His voice was cautious.

"The aliens are coming to steal our sight."

"There are no aliens." I touched her forearm of the hand still holding the lens case, hoping she would grasp reality.

"Yes," she stubbornly replied, turning back to put the case on the counter. Then she unscrewed one of the caps.

"These have to go in your eyes. I read it. They are coming, and we're all going to be blinded so we can't see what they're doing. I'm going to show you how to do it."

Tom nudged me, the sign that it's time to call Dad. "You handle your end, and I'll be right back," he whispered and took off out the door.

Mom turned to me with one of the lenses on her finger.

"Where'd Tommie go?"

"He'll be right back. Let's wait for him."

"No, Honey. We have to get you protected. Now open your eyes wide and . . . "

"Mom," I cut her off and stepped back. "Tom's coming right back. He said to wait for him."

"Don't be afraid." She took my arm and pulled me to her as she bent down to my level. "It's not going to hurt."

I blocked my eyes with my arm.

"Don't you . . . "

"Mom!" Tom cut her off as he ran back up the stairs. "Come on. Let's go down to the dining room."

He tapped me on the shoulder, letting me know that Dad was on his way.

Dropping my arm and backing out of the bathroom, I stood behind him.

"I told you . . . " Mom started to say, but Tom cut her off.

"No, stop. Put it down!" Tom shouted.

There was something about a direct order when she got sick that would snap her into a trancelike state.

"Dad's on the way. Let's go wait for him," he stated firmly.

Her look of determination turned instantly to confusion, and she stood there, lost. Tom took the contact lens off her finger, put it in the case, and then took her by the arm and led her to the dining room table as I followed. We sat there in silence for what seemed like hours.

Fifteen minutes later, Dad relieved us.

As I walked into the living room, I saw a black and white newspaper style magazine on the coffee table. On the front was an iconic image of an oval-faced alien with sinister, cavernous eyes. The headline read, "The Aliens Are Coming After Our Sight."

Mom was committed once again.

* * *

We moved to Jamestown, New York, when I was eight. An ominous feeling started in my gut before we even landed there. The Pearl City, as it was called, was located about 20 miles east of Chautauqua Lake. It was a beautiful old town with a lot of brick roads and old architecture. It was known for its production of pearl ash used for glass products and for the lumber industry. Jamestown became famous for furniture.[2] It's also the birthplace of Lucille Ball.[3] Her museum is located in Celoron, just west of Jamestown and close to the lake.

* * *

Our house had a much different look and setup. There was no view. It had a large yard, and a long driveway led to a two-car garage. A row of rose bushes lined the right-hand side of the driveway.

One day, Dad brought home our first dog.

"He looks like one I had when I was younger," Dad said. "Now listen, he's not allowed inside. Don't get yourselves in trouble." He pointed his finger at each of our noses.

"What're you going to name him?" Mom asked us.

"Well, he came with a name," Dad said, "but you guys can change it if you want."

"What's his name?" I jumped up and down.

"It's Zebbie."

"Zebbie!" We all said it with emphasis. "What kind of name is that?"

"Well, let's get to know him and go from there," Dad suggested. "Help me get him set up."

We headed to the garage and set up a shed with bowls. Outside, Dad pounded a stake into the ground and attached a long chain to it so Zebbie could go in and out of the garage.

"I don't know," I said. "His name kind of fits his look. It's unique. We should keep it. Plus, he knows it already." He looked up at us with his goofy overbite and sweet eyes. He was a Peekaboo with auburn hair, a big ball of fluff.

"Zebbie it is," everyone agreed.

* * *

When Dad started his new job, we rarely saw him and only heard him, and then his angry ways started to escalate.

One night he made it home for dinner. As soon as the four of us heard the car in the driveway, we went silent and started shoveling down our food. When we heard the garage door shut, we collectively paused and listened. It was as if we had telepathy or like someone had yelled "Action!" on a movie set as we got into our roles.

We could rate the darkness of his mood by the way he entered the side door. The screen door retractor was broken, so if you flung it open too hard, it slammed against the house. When Dad was hammered, he always forgot. The door would hit the house, and he'd fumble with whatever he was carrying, all the while cussing up a storm.

After that came the four steps from the entryway to a door that went into a hallway just off the kitchen. If drunk, Dad would somehow hit one of the steps wrong, stumble, catch himself with the door, and then flounder for the handle. He tripped up the steps that night, and we knew he was in a foul mood.

"Where is everyone?" he yelled with a slur.

"In the dining room," Mom answered.

He clomped in and sat down in the chair across from me.

"What's for dinner?" he growled.

"Steak," Mom answered. "You hungry?"

"Already ate."

We were halfway through the meal. Since I was a lean meat eater, I had carved off the fat and grizzle. Dad honed in on me.

"What're you cutting that off for?"

"Don't like it," I said and placed the piece of grizzle off to the side of my plate.

"You eat that."

Not responding, I ate the piece of meat I had just made ready and kept my eyes fixed on my plate.

"You hear me? Pick that up and eat it."

"Steve, leave her alone," Mom pleaded.

"Shut up," he snapped.

Turning back to me, he emphasized each word with a smack of his index finger on the table.

"Do what I said."

Putting it in my mouth, I just held it there.

"I'll sit here all night with you. When your brothers are done, you're going to sit here."

Tom and Todd's eyes didn't leave their plates. They and Mom finished their meals while I sat there, refusing to chew.

"Go get cleaned up for bed," Dad instructed Tom and Todd.

As they pushed back their chairs from the table, they looked at me, pleading with their eyes to just eat it.

"Clear the table, Paula," Dad instructed.

Mom walked back and forth to the kitchen as I sat there holding the piece of ick in my mouth, staring at my hands folded in my lap. Mom took my plate last.

"Honey, just eat it, and then you can go," she said softly.

I swallowed it as she walked away and then sat there for a few more minutes. It was a battle of wills.

"Do what your mom said," Dad said as he put both hands on the table and glared at me.

Opening my mouth, I said, "It's gone."

"You just swallowed it?"

I didn't answer but just looked at his bloodshot, booze-laden eyes.

"Go get yourself ready for bed," he ordered and pointed at the doorway.

Pushing back from the table, I ran.

*

After that, we kids were put on stricter punishments. If one of us got in trouble, we all got punished.

"Keep your noses clean. Don't aggravate your mom. I don't want to be called home all the time," Dad told us.

Todd was the first to slip up. He didn't come home on time for dinner one night, and Tom and I had to go looking for him. We found him playing at a new friend's house past the border where we were allowed to go. Mom was so worried that she told on him, and Dad took the belt to all three of us. He lined us up against the stairwell wall. We knew better than to plead.

"Bend and put your hands on the wall," he ordered.

As we did, we looked to each for support. I was in the middle, and Tom looked to his left at us and mouthed, "Don't cry."

Turning my head to Todd, he mouthed to us, "I'm sorry."

"It's okay," I whispered.

Todd and I silently let the tears flow.

"You get this first because you're the oldest and should have been watching out," Dad shouted.

The first whack sounded, and my head snapped to the right just as Tom winced. His head was down, eyes shut tight, and he was biting his lower lip.

Whack. Whack. Tom got two more.

"You're next for not backing your brother up."

Whack. Whack. It stung so much it made me stop crying.

"You kids will learn." Whack. Todd got his. "You started this."

Dad paused an excruciatingly long time, messing with us.

"Go upstairs to your rooms. Don't come down until you're called."

We practically flew.

Mom came into each of our rooms a bit later.

"I'm sorry, but your brother scared me today. I don't know what I'd do if I lost one of you kids."

We learned to watch each other's backs and cover for one another. But sometimes trouble just couldn't be avoided.

* * *

At some point, one of the rose bushes along the driveway became a problem. Mom wanted it dug out. Tom worked on it for hours trying to get down to the roots. When he finally pulled the stump up, he excitedly yelled, "Hey Mom! Look. I got it."

Todd and I were running through a sprinkler set up in the yard. Mom was sitting in a lawn chair by the driveway. We stopped to check out Tom's accomplishment.

As he yelled to her, he tossed the stump. Mom turned her head to look his way and got clocked right above her eyebrow. It split open immediately. Dad got called, and Mom landed in the emergency room.

Thankfully, accidents didn't count as misbehaving, at least that time, and no one got punished.

* * *

Jolted awake one night by something slamming and then falling, I lay in the dark for a while, petrified because of the yelling and noise. Finally, I crept to my bedroom door and peered across the hallway to my parents' room. The light was on, and the door was open. Tiptoeing to their doorway, I took in the scene.

Dad was in his robe, which was hanging open. His belt was tied loosely under his belly and over his boxer shorts. He was standing over Mom who was on the floor at his feet.

He had pushed her, and she had cracked her head open on the corner of the dresser. The evidence was fresh where her head had hit.

I watched and listened.

"Clean it up," he ordered her.

Mom was naked and on her knees with a bucket of bloody water and a brush. Dad was making her scrub up the pool of blood in the carpet as her wounded head still dripped blood.

"Stop. Just leave me alone, please," she choked out through sobs.

Her hair was disheveled, and blood was running down her face, dripping onto her legs and onto the carpet. Her hands were bloody from scrubbing.

I must have made a noise because Dad snapped his head around and saw me. His eyes were crazy, wild looking. When he focused on my small frame in the doorway, his eyes dilated. He took one big step and loomed over me.

"Is Mom okay?" I asked.

He was sweaty and out of breath, his hair flopping on one side and making him appear rabid.

"I'm okay, Honey. I just fell," Mom said weakly from the background as she tried to rein in her sobs.

"Everything's fine," Dad said. "Go back to bed."

Turning me around, he scooted me off and watched as I crawled into bed and then shut the door.

Scared out of my mind, afraid for Mom's life, I watched the sun rise.

*

When Dad left for work, I peered into the hallway. All was quiet. In my parents' room, the bed was made, everything was picked up, and Mom was nowhere in sight. Standing over the dark stain in the carpet, I knelt down to touch it. It was still damp.

Downstairs, the living room and kitchen were empty. The house seemed deserted. Opening the door to the basement, I heard voices and inched down the stairs to see what was going on.

Mom was in a chair placed backward at the sink with her head tipped back. Tom was washing her hair, tending to the gash on her head. As I rounded the staircase, they both stopped talking and turned to look at me.

"Are you okay, Mom?"

Tom looked at me with wide eyes and nodded his head as if to tell me to go back upstairs.

"I'm fine, Honey. Go upstairs. We'll be up in a minute," Mom told me.

I wondered why she didn't go to the hospital like when she got smacked with the stump. But no one ever talked to me about it. No one said a word.

That night still haunts me.

* * *

Sundays were my favorite because Dad was home, and usually he was in a decent mood and lazy all day, especially during football season. I got to spend time with him. He would be Dad, not scary Dad, although scary Dad was always in the forefront of my mind.

One of his favorite things to do on Sundays was to go to the local butcher and get meats and cheeses and fresh Italian bread so we could make sandwiches. Sometimes, he took me and Todd with him. Afterward, we'd go by the community airport and park at the end of the runway to watch planes take off and land before heading home.

Dad loved airplanes. He'd talk about the mechanics of them and how they'd evolved.

"What did you do in the Navy?" I asked him once.

"I was a gunner. Sat in the belly of the plane and manned the gun."

"What was it like?"

His thoughts would drift off like he was envisioning a memory.

"It was awful to see the people on the ground."

Then his voice trailed off, and his thoughts went somewhere I had no knowledge of.

*

It wasn't until I got older that I realized Sundays were Dad's recovery day after being hung over since Friday night and being out all day on Saturday.

But then Sundays went by the wayside, too. Mom tried to hide it and make excuses, but there were Sundays when Dad didn't come home until Monday after work.

Then he started bringing home tins of cookies and other little gifts to me and Todd.

One Sunday afternoon, he and Todd walked into the kitchen, and Todd handed me a cookie tin.

"These are for you from Lillie," Todd said.

I looked at Dad.

"She's a woman friend of mine," he shrugged.

Mom was standing at the sink doing dishes. The overwhelming sadness on her face as she stared out the window trying to control her quivering chin said it all. The blatant disregard for her in that moment was heartbreaking.

It wasn't hard to figure out that Dad had a new Sunday gig.

* * *

The demise of my parents' 12-year marriage came at Christmastime in 1976 while we were visiting my grandparents in Ohio. Dad took us there and then headed back to Jamestown for "work." It was nice to visit without the tension between my parents, but Mom wasn't doing well. I hoped the reprieve would allow her time to come out of it.

At night, we bunked together in Mom's childhood bedroom. One night, I woke to a strange sound. Silently moving my hand to feel if Mom was in the bed beside me, I turned and looked over at her. The sound was her nails scratching on the headboard over and over again. Laying there stiff as a board, I instinctively knew something was up.

Then she started mumbling.

"Are you okay, Mom?"

"Have you seen my dolly?" Her voice was strange, as if mimicking a little girl. She rambled on and on, but I couldn't understand what she was saying.

I jumped out of bed and ran to Grandma. "Mom's sick again," I panted.

*

Dad returned the next day. He and Mom sat down at my grandparents' dining room table and talked. It was the last time they would ever speak in person.

Then Mom sat me and Todd down.

"I have to get away from your dad if I'm ever going to get better," she told us.

She looked awful.

"Can we stay with you?" I cried.

"Not now, Honey. I have to get better. You and Toddy are going to stay with your father for now. Tommie's staying here with me."

Sobbing, I ran to Tom, and we held each other.

"When are you coming home?" Todd asked, teary-eyed.

"I don't know, Honey, but I'll see you kids soon."

She didn't promise. I caught it.

Then Dad walked into the room.

"We leave tomorrow. I have to be at work on Monday."

*

The next day, he packed us up, and off we went, bawling as we pulled away. Todd and I were on our knees in the back seat looking out the rear window to catch our last glimpse of Mom, Tom, and Zebbie, with no clue what was going to happen or when we were going to get to see each other again.

It was a Sunday.

*

Trips in the car always sucked, but that ride was the most excruciating. Staring out the window, I tried to control my crying so I wouldn't get in trouble, and I didn't dare ask to have the window down to get rid of the sickening cigarette smoke.

Eventually, Dad broke the silence.

"Things are going to change. Your Aunt Toots is coming to help us out. Give me time to figure things out. I want you kids on your best behavior."

It was shocking that someone from Dad's side of the family was coming. It was also a rare occasion that Dad addressed us kids.

Trips in the car most often involved Dad talking about things along the way, stuff about the surrounding area, cars, and trucks, but he would only address Tom or Todd. This time, Tom wasn't there, so when I asked a question, Dad said, "What do you think, Todd?" Then the two of them had a conversation about my question.

In the back seat, I was just a girl wondering why I didn't matter.

* * *

Back in Jamestown, Aunt Toots was waiting for us. She was my favorite of Dad's sisters and a welcome sight. I ran into her arms.

"You okay?" she asked into the top of my head.

"Don't know. Scared. What's going to happen?"

"Don't know, Babe. I don't know."

She pulled Todd into our hug. When she let us go, she said, "You kids go on upstairs and let me talk to your dad." Her tone had changed into stern annoyance.

When Dad called us back down to the living room, he was waiting at the base of the stairs. In his hands were a couple of small, perfectly wrapped gifts.

"Come. Sit down on the couch, and open these."

His mood had changed to almost giddy like he had a surprise for two little children. Oh, we were two children all right, and he had a surprise.

"These are for you two from Lillie." His smile was nauseating. Todd and I just stood there with the gifts in our hands.

"Open them," he encouraged us.

Mine was in a small box. Todd's was in a round tin. We looked at each other and started unwrapping them. It felt like I was moving through slime. Todd finished first, popped open the tin, and found cookies.

He and Dad watched as I opened the small black box. Inside was a gold ring with a pink stone. Wanting to throw up on it, I set it down on the coffee table instead.

Dad pulled us close to him, something he rarely ever did, especially with me. Then he dropped a bomb.

"We're going to make some changes now. Lillie has offered to let us stay with her. That's what we're doing."

He already had it all planned out.

"She's going to give us a call in just a bit. I want you to speak to her . . . " he nudged me, ". . . and introduce yourself. Thank her for the beautiful ring."

Sliding down off the couch to head up to my room, I caught sight of Aunt Toots in the doorway. She had been listening to our conversation, and the look on her face matched my feeling of nausea. Just as I hit the first step, the phone rang.

"Let's go. That's probably her," Dad said.

Dad jumped off the couch and waved us into the kitchen. Then he handed me the phone.

"Say hello to Lillie." That puke-worthy smile was back.

I had no idea what to say to the woman. "Hello," I squeezed out.

"Hi. I'm so excited to meet you," she cheerfully told me. "I'm looking forward to you guys coming."

"Thank you, and thank you for the ring." It was a polite grit through my teeth.

3

On my knees again in the back seat of the car, we pulled out of the driveway. I watched as our house faded in the distance, the last remnants of our family life gone. When we moved to the other side of town, I was 11. Todd and I had each packed a bag, and Dad told us the rest would come later.

On the ride to our "new adventure," as Dad called it, he excitedly talked with Todd who had graduated to the front seat.

"This is going to be a good change. You'll see. You'll have a new school, make new friends."

We each sat quietly, looking out our respective windows. Change was needed, but it seemed like we were in another reality.

Once we went past Allen Park, it was unknown territory. We could've been in another state. Eventually, we started down a long avenue.

"Coming up on your right is where you'll go to school next year. I'm not going to pull you kids out right now," Dad said after several lights.

"How are we going to get there?" Todd asked.

"Either Lillie or I will drop you off, Traci." He addressed me as he looked through the rearview mirror. "When you get out of school, you're going to go over to Julie's house, Lillie's oldest. She lives down the street, so you'll walk there. Now we're coming into your new neighborhood. Lillie's is midway down the hill," Dad informed us as we started the descent.

"This is us." He slowed and turned into a driveway at the side of a ranch-style house painted slate blue with white trim.

Not wanting to delay the inevitable, I stepped out of the car to look around. The house was on a corner surrounded by a large yard. Next to the driveway was a huge crab tree. Between the tree and the sidewalk was a wooden sign painted white with black lettering and staked into the ground. It read, "Lillie's Beauty Shop."

"Let's go," Dad said.

As we rounded the side of the house, it opened up into a big front yard with several trees. There was a picnic table under a massive oak. We walked toward the entryway past a waist-high, white picket fence that enclosed the front porch and entered through the gate. Dad knocked.

Standing there awkward and scared, not knowing what to expect, I thought about Mom and wondered if she was okay and what she was doing. I wondered what Tom was doing and whether he and Mom missed us.

The door opened, and we were greeted with a drawn out "Hi . . . i . . . i . . . i. I've been waiting to meet you!"

She headed straight for me, stooped down to my level, and cupped my face in her hands. "I'm Lil. It's so nice to finally meet you." She smiled with stained teeth into my face. Her breath reeked of cigarette smoke.

She bounced over to Todd. "Hi, Toddy. You ready for some cookies?"

"Yes," he said excitedly.

Standing up, Lill greeted Dad, grasping his arm and pulling him in close for a kiss.

"Hi, Steve," she said in a sultry voice.

I tried to remember the last time I saw Dad kiss anyone, and I wondered if he had ever hit her.

"Come," she told us. "Come inside and make yourselves comfortable."

We stepped into the living room. Her house smelled amazing, like an Italian kitchen with fresh simmering sauce. I could make out the aroma of each vegetable, herb, and spice because they hadn't comingled yet. There was onion, garlic, basil, and thyme.

A little white poodle bounded up to me and started licking my leg.

"Go, Missy," Lil shooed her away.

Looking around the square living room, the first item that caught my attention was an organ on the far wall. Lil caught me.

"Would you like to play it sometime?"

I nodded my head yes.

"This one doesn't talk, Steve?"

She kept her eyes on me but addressed Dad. It was a challenge, a warning.

"She does!" He shot me a look.

"Yes, I'd like to play sometime," I responded dryly.

"All right, then. Are you kids hungry?"

"Yes!" Todd answered for us.

"The table's set up in here because I'm having some work done in the kitchen so we have more room for a breakfast table in there." She waved her hand to indicate a card table that was set up with a cloth over it. "I have the formal dining table already set for dinner tomorrow with my family. Are you kids pasta eaters?"

"Yes!" Todd answered for us again.

"Sit, sit," she invited as she stepped into the kitchen. "Steve, will you make us a drink?"

"Sure," Dad responded, standing back up.

Taking a few steps, he opened a door with shutters. Inside was a liquor cabinet that he seemed very familiar with. Pulling out a few bottles and grabbing a couple of glasses, Dad headed into the kitchen.

Dad never drank at home when we lived with Mom. She didn't drink. And he never interacted with Mom the way he did with Lil. I wondered how long their affair had been going on.

The kitchen was large, with the refrigerator, sink, and a lot of cupboards and counter space on the right and the stove and more storage on the left. There were pots simmering and steaming on every burner. The far wall was torn up, and some cupboards had been removed. It was a bright and airy space painted light blue and white with flowered wallpaper on one wall.

The living room was nicely decorated and comfortable. High shuttered windows on the surrounding walls and a large picture window on the entrance wall allowed for plenty of natural lighting. There was a small TV on a bookshelf and a desk area to the left where the phone was.

Lil returned with oven mitts on and carrying a large roasting pan. She placed it in the center of the table.

"This is beef braciola with orecchiette," she said and then removed the lid.

The most scrumptious waft of goodness hit the air. With no idea what it was or how to say what she said, I couldn't wait to try it.

"Be right back," she told us and then returned to the kitchen only to reemerge with a basket of freshly baked bread.

Dad came in behind her carrying two drinks.

They sat down, and Lil said, "Let's pray."

Todd and I looked at each other. We didn't know how. Lil and Dad had folded their hands in front of them. Their heads were down, and their eyes were closed. We followed suit but kept one eye on Lil.

"Thank You, Lord, for this food and for bringing us together for this meal. In Jesus's name, Amen."

*

"Let's eat," Dad said.

Lil grabbed my plate and loaded it up with piping hot braciola. It reminded me of Baba's pigs-in-a-blanket because of the rolls, but it was completely different. The braciola was meat stuffed with something and soaked in red sauce. It was served on a bed of small noodles. Lil set the plate in front of me.

"Eat your salad first, and let that cool down," she directed. Then her tone changed, and she shot me an annoyed look. "First, get that hair out of your face. Do something with it."

My hair was long and a bit unruly since Mom wasn't around to help me with it. It was down, and some stray strands were the focus of her annoyance, so I brushed them back and dug in.

"Steve, they don't know prayer?" Lil asked. She had caught both of us watching her.

"No, their mother and I didn't attend church together."

"Well, that's going to change." She looked at each of us individually. "We'll go to my church as a family. Were they ever baptized?"

"Oh yes, they both were."

"What's that mean?" I shyly asked.

"After you kids were born, your mother and I had you blessed."

"What does that mean?" Todd chimed in.

"It means you were sprinkled with the blood of Jesus so He watches over you," Lil explained. "You'll learn all that. In the meantime, now that you're here, I'll get you doing some chores. We'll start with dishes after dinner. Todd, you can help me clear the table, and you'll do the dishes." Lil pointed at me as she took a sip of her drink. "After that, I'll show you your rooms and get you settled in."

Dad kept his eyes fixed on his plate.

*

Dinner was interrupted by the sound of doors opening. Someone was coming in from somewhere, and then there were loud, fast footsteps on stairs, two at a time.

A tall young man stepped into the doorway of the living room from around the corner of the kitchen. He was in jeans, a T-shirt, and a winter jacket that hung open. His thumbs were hooked to his front pockets. His hair was black in an afro style, and he had a cocky smile with a big dimple in his chin.

"Hey," he nodded at all of us.

The look of irritation on Lil's face was priceless, so I gave him a big smile.

"This is my son, Jimmy," she introduced him. "He was supposed to be out for the night." She shot him a snotty look.

"Just had to stop in for somethin'. Hi, Steve," Jimmy waved with a bounce.

His mannerisms reminded me of Ted Logan.[1] Jimmy turned and loped through the kitchen.

"He graduates in June," Lil told us. "He'll be out of the house soon."

"How long has he known Dad?"

"Eat your dinner and sit up," Lil told me.

Jimmy reappeared with a drawstring bag of clothes in his hand.

"I'm taking off," he waved and then disappeared around the corner, thudding down the stairs two at a time, slamming doors behind him. A giggle squeaked out of me, and Lil shot me a glare.

"Let's finish up and get these dishes cleared," she said as she stood up and took her plate.

Dad sucked down the last of his drink and then stood up and followed her.

"You ready for another?" he asked.

"Yes."

Wondering if she was as mean a drunk as Dad, I prepared myself mentally, picked up my half-finished plate of food, and headed into the kitchen.

"Use the dishwasher for dishes and silverware only. Pots, pans, and cooking utensils get washed and dried. Todd, when you're done clearing the table, start drying."

Dad handed her another drink and then walked back into the living room with his.

Lil stood behind me, watching.

After I loaded a few dishes, she gave a loud "tsk."

"You're so inept," she hissed in my ear. "This is how you load a dishwasher."

She bent down to rearrange what I had loaded. It was almost as if she were taunting to see if she could get a rise out of me, like it was some kind of a mean game that gave her a thrill.

"Finish up," she snapped and walked into the living room.

"Is she always this mean?" I whispered to Todd.

He just looked at me with big eyes as if to say, *Is this really happening?*

We finished up and reported for inspection. Todd had left a few items on the counter to ask where to put them, but before he could explain, he got reprimanded.

"Now, let's get you both into your rooms and settled in. It's almost time for bed. Come with me," Lil said.

We followed her out the kitchen, into the dining room, and down a hallway.

Midway down, she pointed. "Traci, you're in here," and she flipped on the light. "And Todd, you're right here across the hall. Steve!" she yelled out, "did you bring their things in?"

We walked into our respective bedrooms. Pleasantly surprised, mine was big with a little entryway and a large closet off to the left. The bed was positioned in the middle of the wall with a nightstand on either side. There was a dresser and a desk against the opposite wall that adjoined the kitchen.

I walked around the bed to look out the window into the night. That spot would become my confessional safe place.

"Wow! Your room's big," Todd said as he walked in.

"This used to be my Mary Jane's room. You'll meet her tomorrow. Todd's room was Jimmy's when he was young, but he's in the back room now, which used to be Julie's, my oldest. She'll be here with her family tomorrow, too."

"Will Jimmy be here?" He reminded me of Tom, whom I missed terribly.

"He'll show up at some point. You never know with him."

"Let me see your room, Todd." We ran across the hall. His room was much smaller, rectangle shaped with a small closet, twin bed, a nightstand, and a dresser.

"Here's your bags." Dad had shown up.

"The bathroom's down here at the end of the hall around the corner," Lil said as she walked down to show us. "Who's bathing first?"

"Me," I offered.

"I'll get it running. You get situated."

*

Unpacking my things felt strange and out of place, as if I'd been transported. It was like looking at a picture of my family and watching the images dissolve and float away only to be replaced by some other unknown family. It felt like I was in a play but didn't know my role.

Staring out at the neighborhood with the lights shining off the icy brick street below, I noticed another driveway that was much lower than the other one because of the slope of the yard. That's where Jimmy came in, I thought.

"Get in! I'll be right there to help you," Lil yelled out the order.

"I can wash myself!" I shot back.

Grabbing my pj's, I headed for the bathroom and hopped into the tub.

Lil came bursting through the door.

"We only have one bathroom, so get moving. Hurry up. Let me see how you wash yourself." She tossed a washcloth at me.

I was mortified. She stood there staring at me. Soaking the cloth, I soaped it up and started on a leg first, trying to keep myself covered up.

"Oh Jesus Christ, let's go," she snapped as she situated the bathmat and knelt down. "That's not how you bathe yourself." She grabbed the washcloth. "You start from the top down." She shoved the cloth in my face and scrubbed. "I'm telling you right now, we're going to do something about this hair. Rinse your face."

Then she quickly and roughly scrubbed my neck, chest, and tummy. "Now stand up," she ordered. "Rinse the cloth out before washing your private parts." She demonstrated, resoaped, and handed it to me. "Wash."

Embarrassed, my hand barely moved.

"Do you always tickle yourself like that?"

Grabbing the cloth, she held my arm and forced her hand between my legs. I let out a little cry because it hurt.

"Oh stop," she shook me by the arm. "Now sit down, finish scrubbing, and rinse off. Then drain the water, and stand up."

Hurrying, I did as she said, and then she tossed me a towel.

"Dry off, head to toe. Let's go. Todd's up next."

Quickly complying, I put my jammies on.

"Go, say good night to your father, and get in bed."

Walking into the kitchen, I stood in the doorway to the living room. Dad was asleep in a chair, snoring loudly, his drink still in hand.

Tiptoeing around the corner to see where Jimmy had come in, I opened the door and peered down at a dark stairway to a basement. Then quietly shutting the door, I went to my room and hopped into bed, Missy by my side.

The wall at my headboard adjoined the bathroom. I listened as Lil instructed Todd on how to wash his private parts. I stared out the window into the night.

Mom and Tom were my only thoughts as I cried myself to sleep.

* * *

It had been a week since we left Ohio, and already it was another world. Waking the next morning, I wondered what the day was going to bring. Studying my new room, I decided that if it was going to be my space, then it needed my touch. David Cassidy was going up first.

"Wake up, kids! Get the table set!" Reality hit with Lil pounding on both our doors.

The smell of bacon was in the air as I schlepped out of bed. Whatever happens, I thought, at least we'll be well fed.

Dad was cooking. I'd never seen him cook, only on the grill.

Todd came in behind me and gasped.

"Whoa! You cook, Dad?"

"I cook," he laughed. He had a great laugh. And when he laughed really hard, he wheezed like Muttley.[2]

But then he tapped Lil on the butt as she walked by and said, "Things will be different. You'll see," and it spoiled the moment.

"Here are napkins." Lil shoved them into my hand. "Grab silverware, salt, pepper, butter. Hurry up."

We could never move fast enough for Lil.

After we sat down to eat, Lil said a prayer.

"Who is Jesus?" I asked.

"The Son of God. God created us."

"How did He create us?"

"That's . . . you'll learn all that. We give thanks for what we're provided. For now, let's eat." She cut off the conversation. "After breakfast, I'll take you downstairs and show you how to work the washer and dryer." She looked at both of us and then shoved a forkful of potato and eggs into her mouth.

* * *

Julie and her family arrived first for Sunday dinner. She resembled her mom and wore her hair short, similar to Lil's. But in contrast to Lil's brown eyes, Julie had crystal blue eyes with amazing, thick, long, dark lashes. She was short and somewhat squat. Her husband, Ric, was good looking and short in stature as well.

Mary Jane was next. She resembled her mom in a completely different way with long, thick, dark hair and dark chocolate eyes. Extremely thin and a bit taller than her sister, she had an amazing smile that was a bit crooked. She was hyper and jittery like she'd drunk a pot of coffee. She didn't sit for long and paced back and forth a lot.

Jimmy showed up last and was late. As he greeted his sisters, they razzed one another and seemed to be tight.

As each one of Lil's kids came in, they greeted Dad by name as if they'd known him for a while, especially Mary Jane.

"Do you know my dad?" I asked after he had introduced us.

"Oh yes, Doll," Mary Jane answered. "I've known him a long time. We met where I bartend. I'm the one who introduced him to my mom." She gave me a big smile and then lit a cigarette.

I wanted to scream in her face and tell her he's married and has his own family—but I didn't.

*

Once we all sat down for dinner, Julie spoke to me from across the table as she lit a cigarette. "Are you excited to come visit me?"

"Yes, thank you." It was polite, but what I really wanted to ask was if this insta-family thing seemed odd to her, because to me it felt like *The Twilight Zone*.[3] She gave me a sympathizing look, so I must not have kept the confusion and frustration off my face very well.

"Hey!" Jimmy threw a wadded-up piece of napkin at me. He was a nervous guy like his sister, one leg constantly shaking. It was like having motion sickness around him.

"I think I went to school with your brother," he said.

"Tom, his name is Tom," I answered.

"Yeah. I haven't seen him around. Where'd he go?"

"He's in Ohio with my mom." I sounded sad.

He stared at me a moment and then said, "It gets better. My mom's been divorced twice."

"Where's your dad?"

"He lives on the other side of town not too far from Julie."

"How old were you when they got divorced?"

"Six. I've been going back and forth for years, but I'm almost out of here."

"Where are you going?"

"Mary Jane's getting ready to head out to Colorado. I'm thinking about following her."

Just then I was summoned into the kitchen.

"Come serve these dishes," Lil ordered.

While carrying the food to the table, I listened in on conversations.

Mary Jane had a friend who was injured in a Jeep accident and was wearing a halo brace. Once he was able to travel, she was going to help him back to Colorado and was staying there. She hoped to be gone by April. She was excited for an upcoming Manfred Mann[4] concert.

Jimmy had a friend named Terry in Colorado that he was hoping to bunk up with.

Julie was assuring Dad that watching us was not an inconvenience.

By the time I sat down again, I had delivered salad, a huge bowl of spaghetti partially sauced as instructed so it wouldn't stick, a bowl of sauce, another of meatballs and sausage, and finally a basket of warm, homemade bread.

"Let's say prayer. Jimmy, do it," Lil announced, sitting down.

Bowing my head but one-eying the room, Lil's head was down with her hands in her lap.

Julie's head was lowered, and her forearms were splayed in front of her plate with her hands steepled in the center. Ric had his arm across the back of Julie's chair and was leaning in toward her with his head down.

Mary Jane looked straight forward with her eyes closed and brought her hands together, fingers to her lips.

Dad's head was bowed with his hands resting on the table.

Todd was eyeing the room, too. We caught each other and elbow-nudged one another.

Jimmy had his hands clasped, resting on his forehead, head down.

"Thank you for these good eats, Lord. Amen."

It was quick and to the point, and then everyone dug in.

"Are you guys Italian?" I generally inquired after the noise died down.

"And Portuguese," Jimmy answered as he slurped in some noodles.

"James," Lil said sternly.

He laughed and bobbed his head.

"My dad's Italian. Lil's Portuguese."

"What's that?"

"Same as Italian, only meaner."

"Jim," Mary Jane snapped and giggled. Julie laughed, too.

"Kids!" Lil snapped.

"What? Just giving them a heads up if they haven't already figured it out." It was a snicker from Jimmy followed by a cocky snort.

Dad was buried in his plate.

"Enough!" Lil shot a look at everyone. It stopped my breathing, thinking the table might flip.

"Truth hurts," Jimmy snortled and started shoveling pasta into his face.

For as stern as Lil was, Jimmy's table manners sure missed out. Things settled down, and we got through dinner, but the tension was thick between Lil and Jimmy. Julie and Mary Jane volunteered to help clear the table for dessert, so the rest of us were dismissed. I followed Jimmy to his room.

"Can I ask you something?" I said.

"Make it quick. Don't let her catch you talking to me."

"What you're saying—what do you mean?"

"You're going to have to get tough. Life with her isn't easy. Julie and Mary Jane ran away once they had enough. I've been hanging in, but she'll kick me out the door soon."

"Where will you go?"

Someone was coming down the hall, so I quickly backed out of his doorway and went into the bathroom.

"Jim, you gotta cool your jets. You're going to scare those poor kids." It was Mary Jane. She was the only one who called him Jim.

"They should be scared."

"Well, stop. You never know. Maybe this will be good."

"It's never good."

After she walked away, I softly opened the door and stepped out.

"I'll go to my dad's." Jimmy winked at me. "You better get back out there."

4

Dad's thing was to call her Lillie. To me and Todd, she was just Lil—one syllable, like the word *witch*.

Lil consistently nagged at Todd and me about "our laziness." She belittled us and said how awful it was that we didn't know how to do chores. We tried to do everything we were told, but it was never enough. It's not that we didn't know how; we needed to learn things to Lil's specifications.

Her motto was this: "You're in my house."

* * *

A couple weeks in, Todd and I walked into her kitchen for breakfast and got hit with a new one.

"You kids drink too much milk. I'm not going to be your milk bank just so it will be like you lived before," she smacked at us as we sat down to eat a bowl of cereal.

"And that's the last of those cereals you'll eat. You get what I buy."

"What's a milk bank?" I asked.

"Your father had to pay off a huge milk bill. There's no delivery man at this house, and I'm not paying for you two to drink milk." She kept emphasizing the word *milk* like it was something detestable.

About a week later, we rounded the corner for breakfast. Lil was sitting at the table in the area that had just been completed. Looking up at us over her reading glasses, she watched as Todd grabbed two bowls and I headed to the fridge.

"Looking for your milk? It's not in there. Your milk's up here now."

She stood and took out a box from the cupboard behind her and slammed it down on the counter.

"Instant Dry Milk," I read after Todd handed it to me.

"Read the instructions. You mix it with water," Lil told us.

Todd and I met eyes with a look that said, *This isn't going to be good.*

"These," Lil snapped, "are the cereals you'll eat." She slammed down two boxes.

We both tried, but neither of us could hack the taste of the powdered milk. It was like watered down homemade glue. With the Shredded Wheat we were provided, it tasted like wet grassland. The generic Puffed Wheat was no better. The combination was like chewing on wet Styrofoam popcorn.

We opted for toast and fruit. As we grew older and started earning money through chores and side jobs, if we wanted milk, we had to buy it ourselves.

* * *

My first visit to Julie's house was uncomfortable and awkward. While her home was beautiful, there was a sadness there. After she let me in, she sat back down to her cup of coffee and already lit cigarette.

"Are you doing okay with everything?" she asked, taking a drag.

Shucking my coat, I laid it over one of the chairs. Not knowing what to say, I just left it alone and sat down in the dining room chair across from her.

"Would you like some hot chocolate?"

"Yes, please."

How did they know that the way to get me to open my mouth was usually by way of food or something sweet?

"Come, help me make it."

"Can I ask you something?"

"You can ask me anything."

"Why is your mom so mean?" It just blurted out of me.

Julie laughed. She laughed so hard she had to put her cigarette down.

"Why do you guys think it's so funny that she's mean?" It irritated me.

"Oh, Honey, we aren't laughing because it's funny. It's crazy. It only gets funny when you're finally out of the house."

"Jimmy told me you ran away."

"Yes, and I never looked back."

"But you get along with her now?"

"Well, I tolerate her until she takes it to the point where I leave and go home. It's a roller coaster ride that you'll have to get off eventually."

* * *

"Put your shoulders back." That rang in my ears at least three times a day. "You need to learn to do something with that hair, or I'm cutting it off" was a warning I heard just as many times.

Headed in from playing one day, I was a mess after rolling around in leaves and climbing trees. Bits of nature were all over me, especially in my hair.

Coming in through the basement, I tried to make it quietly up the stairs to clean myself up before anyone saw me.

"Who's in?" Lil yelled from behind the stairs where she kept her salon supplies.

"It's me."

Crap! Stopping instantly, I tried to comb my fingers through my hair.

"What are you doing?"

"Heading in to get cleaned up for dinner."

It was a lie and not a good one either because dinner wasn't for several hours. She came around the corner and stood at the base of the steps, looking up at me. "Jesus Christ! Come down here. Let's go!"

Into her salon we went.

"Sit," she pointed.

There was no fighting it, so I just stayed silent.

She buttoned a cape around my neck and swung me around. The chair back released, and I breathed in the stink of a mixture of cigarettes and hair spray off her shirt as she roughly washed my hair without saying a word.

"This crap's like a rat's nest," she spit at me in the mirror after pushing me back up.

She sprayed detangler and proceeded to tear a comb through until I cried out in pain. Then she eased up a bit.

Watching as she chopped my hair off, I let the tears flow.

* * *

Whatever Dad saw in Lil, she made him happy—in the beginning at least. He was more approachable, came home every night after work, and cooked dinner most nights. He made homemade salad dressings and Serbian meals, and the house often smelled like Baba's.

But every night, Todd and I were trapped in their booze-infested melodrama. The same scene played every night, just with different action. Lil usually drank martinis, and Dad's favorite was a Manhattan—several of them.

Lil started drinking before her workday even ended. She'd often still have clients for a couple of hours after Dad got home from work, so he'd get dinner started, make her some drinks, and take them down to her while she finished out the day.

Our dinner hour was around 7:30 p.m., sometimes later, and I dreaded sitting down at the table. By that time, they were both numb from alcohol. They'd be bobble-headed and slurring their words, ready to pick at me and Todd or argue with each other while we sat there listening.

By the time dinner was over, they were usually pissed off at each other. Lil would clean up and go to bed. Dad would clean up and come into the living room where Todd and I were trying to enjoy the hour of TV we were allowed. He'd get comfortable in his favorite chair and fall asleep within minutes, snoring loudly. It was so annoying.

Cooking put Dad in a good mood, at least until he got through his second drink. Catching him at the right moment was key. While he was preparing chicken paprikash one night, I approached him.

"When do we get to talk to Mom?" It had been almost two months.

"Not until we get some things settled between us. It should be soon."

"Dad," I paused.

"Yeah, Honey."

He looked down at me and knew that when I said Dad like that, something touchy was going to follow. He seemed to find it humorous at times when I found my voice.

"Why is Lil so mean?" I asked. "You see how she treats us but never say anything."

"Just try to stay out of her way. Don't make waves. Get to know her."

The day she cut my hair, though, he was pissed and gave me the most pitiful look.

"That's a little extreme," he scolded Lil.

"She was warned," she shot back.

"I don't care. Don't you do anything like that again. You talk to me before you do something with my kids."

"You don't get to tell me what to do in my house. Those kids are lucky you didn't put them up for adoption, and they should be grateful to have a roof over their heads."

"You're out of line!" he said.

The look he shot Lil shut her up, and she stormed off.

"Go to your room," he ordered me.

* * *

Jimmy came and went a lot. He was rarely around, and there was always drama when he was home. He showed up one night at just the wrong time. Lil was in a foul mood and at the end of her third drink.

"You have a lot of nerve coming here," she laid into him, stopping him in the kitchen by standing in front of him.

"What is it now?" he snorted down at her. He liked to rile her up.

"The bag of pot in your closet. Is that what you came for? You're done living here. I want you out, completely out."

"Cool. Can I get my stuff?"

She stepped aside.

"Go to your room," she ordered me.

After a few minutes, I tiptoed down the hall to Jimmy's room. He was throwing his things into bags.

"You're not coming back, huh?"

"I'll be around for a little while. This isn't anything new. I'll say goodbye before heading to Colorado." He brushed me on the cheek with his finger as he walked past me. "Hang in there, kid."

* * *

Todd and I learned to do chores Lil's way. Saturdays were cleaning days. Dad and Lil spent most of the day running errands or golfing. We spent the day as grunts.

Chores came first in Lil's house, but when they were gone, we had the run of the place, screwing around and watching wrestling. But we quickly learned that we had to be very vigilant because we got sloppy once.

"What got done today?" Lil asked us when they got home.

"I started the laundry. We dusted and vacuumed," I answered.

"Did you vacuum under the furniture?"

"Yes," we collectively fibbed.

"Let's see."

She walked directly over to the couch. Unbeknownst to us, she had put a neat little pile of dirt under it that she took from one of the houseplants. We got dinged and had to do the vacuuming again.

Todd and I looked at each other like the crazy train had just derailed. We did not make that mistake a second time.

* * *

Dad called us into the living room one Saturday afternoon.

"Sit down. I want to talk to you two for a minute." It was a serious tone that put us on guard. "I know this hasn't been easy on you kids. I know you miss your mom."

Duh, I wanted to say. *I've asked to talk to her just about every night!*

"You know your Mom and I are getting divorced." He looked at each of us individually. He never told either of us that directly, but we knew and nodded yes.

"We've worked things out between us," he said next. "Are you ready to give your mom a call?"

"Yes!" We yelled simultaneously, jumping up and down.

"Go call her." He handed me a piece of paper with a phone number on it and pointed to the phone.

"Hello."

The sound of her voice broke me, and I started crying.

"Oh, Honey, don't cry. I'm okay. It's so good to hear your voice."

"I miss you, Mom! I'm just crying because I'm happy to finally talk to you."

"I know. I miss you, too," and she started crying.

"Is Tom there?" I asked.

"He's right here, Honey, waiting to talk to you. I'll give you to him for a minute while I collect myself."

"Hi, Babe," Tom said in my ear.

It was so good to hear his voice, and I just sobbed.

"Don't cry. I'm here. We've been waiting to talk to you guys. How's Todd?"

"He's right here," I choked out. "Here. Talk to him."

"Hi, Tom," Todd excitedly yelled and proceeded to talk his ear off. Todd talked to Mom and then handed the phone back to me.

"You okay, Honey?" Mom asked.

"Yeah. It's just been so long. I've been waiting."

"I know. But now we'll talk regularly. What have you been doing?"

We caught up, and then I spoke with Tom.

"You guys doing okay?" he said in that special way as if to say, *What's really going on?*

"Yes and no. Can't really say right now."

Dad was sitting on the couch, and Lil was right around the corner in the kitchen.

"Well, we can talk whenever now. You can call anytime. It doesn't have to be just weekly. Try to call me when you can talk, okay?"

"Okay. When are we going to see you?"

"Don't know that yet. I'm working on getting my driver's license. Hang in there for me, okay?"

I committed their phone number to memory. It was a relief to finally be able to confide in Tom and let it out because there was no one else to tell.

* * *

Awakened by a loud crash one night, I jumped out of bed to look out the window. The basement lights were on. That's where it sounded like it came from, so I got down and put my ear against the heater vent in the floor.

"I hate you, Steve. Keep your goddamn hands off me," Lil was screaming.

Then came a smack. He hit her, and it was a doozy. They were in the basement hallway.

"Get away from me." She was defiant.

Someone got shoved into the wall, and I heard another smack.

Lil cried out in pain and screamed, cussing at him. Then she ran up the stairs, past my room and into hers, slamming and locking the door.

Minutes of silence went by, and I wondered if Todd was awake. Sometimes, he could sleep through anything.

Dad banged on their bedroom door, which almost sent me flying off my bed.

He banged again and called to her.

"Go, Steve. The police are on the way."

This was something new.

One of the kitchen chairs scraped the floor. They were heavy, made of iron, so it was obvious anytime someone moved them. I assumed Dad sat down.

In the waiting that night, the silence was loud. Then I heard the sirens from the distance, growing louder as they approached. They cut out about a block away, and a few seconds later, red and blue strobes started dancing on the walls of my room.

I slipped out of bed and looked out the window. I watched as two cruisers pulled into the lower driveway. The lights came on in the neighbors' houses across the street.

Nothing had changed, and everything had changed.

My heart jumped when Lil pounded on both our doors.

"Let's go, kids. Come outside with me."

Hurtling over the bed, I opened the door just as Todd came out of his. We gave each other the I-got-you look, held hands, and followed Lil out the dining room door.

Sneaking a look back, I saw Dad sitting at the kitchen table, bent over with his head in his hands.

The three of us walked through the yard and around the side of the house where it sloped down beside the garage. At the top of the small hill, Lil instructed us to sit down. Then she proceeded to the driveway.

The neighbors next to us opened their door slightly, peered out, and then quickly shut it.

"Where is he?" one of the officers asked Lil.

"I think he's in the kitchen."

We were sitting on the grass in our pajamas and bare feet when the other officer headed toward us.

"You kids okay? You're not hurt?"

"No," we answered as one.

"All right, sit tight."

Knocking on the screen door to the dining room, the officer yelled, "You okay in there, sir? All right. I'm gonna come in. You stay seated right where you are, okay?"

Lil and the other officer had gone into the basement.

Huddled together, Todd and I waited as more of the neighbors looked out their windows or opened their doors.

Maybe 10 minutes went by, and then the policeman, Dad, Lil, and the other officer emerged from the garage.

"That's what we like to see," one of the policemen said, "when folks work it out. You both have a good night now. Don't have us back out here."

"It won't happen again," Dad politely responded and waved.

"Let's go, kids. Come on," he called to us. "Get upstairs and back into bed."

*

No one ever spoke about that night until one evening after dinner. Lil dismissed Todd and told him she'd help me with the dishes.

"Did you know about your dad's violence?" She stood beside me and waited.

"Yes."

She signaled for me to go on.

"He used to beat my mom terribly."

"Why haven't you ever spoken up about it?"

"It's . . . not talked about. Figured you'd find out for yourself."

"Not with me, not in my house. I grew up in that crap," she huffed and walked off to take a bath, leaving me with the rest of the cleanup.

*

"Lil, where were you raised?" I asked while doing some baking one night.

"Harrisburg, Pennsylvania. My Aunt Viv raised me."

"Why your aunt?"

She turned to me with her hands on her hips and sighed. Something in her demeanor collapsed for a moment, so I stopped mixing and gave her my full attention.

"When my sister Mary and I were young, our father killed our mom." She paused and clenched her jaw. There was no emotion. We just stared into each other's eyes as if we could watch what she was saying play out.

"A fight broke out between them one night," she explained. "It was one of many nights. But that night, I grabbed Mary's hand, and we ran into the closet. Mom tried to avoid him, but he caught her arm. We thought she was dead when she hit the wall. He beat her and choked her. She fought hard." Lil's voice trailed off a bit. "Suddenly, he had a knife, and he stabbed—and didn't stop."

Lil blinked. The clip was over, and we were back in the kitchen.

Having lived in fear that Dad would kill Mom, I understood her on that level.

"Is that why your treatment of people can be so harsh at times?" It was brave, but I was hoping to catch her in a vulnerable moment. It didn't work.

She shifted her eyes at me and glibly responded, "Jesus came to me and told me I was doing well by you kids."

No words came, but I shot her an incredulous look because I couldn't help it. She stomped off to take a bath.

Looking out the kitchen window into the night and still not knowing who Jesus was, it didn't feel like He was on our side.

* * *

The next time Dad put his hands on Lil, things really went south for him. Lil went into full-on mob style right back at him.

It was in the evening as it usually was. Todd and I were in bed. Lil had bathed. It started in their bedroom as I lay on my bed listening through the wall. Dad must have tried to get frisky.

"No, Steve. You're drunk."

"Don't push me away, Babe," he persisted.

"I said don't."

Someone got shoved and hit the wall, knocking stuff to the ground.

"Don't you . . . "

Smack!

"You're going to regret that," Lil screamed.

She ran down the hall, through the kitchen, and down the basement steps.

Dad gave up and went into the bathroom. For about the next 10 minutes, he did his thing on the other side of the wall and then got in the shower.

Like lightning, headlights flashed across my room and then quickly went out. A car door slammed, and the garage door opened. Dropping to the floor, I listened from the vent.

"Where is he?" someone said sternly. Recognizing the voice, I popped up to glance out at the car. It was Ric.

"He's upstairs. Take care of it. I'm not putting up with this."

"Stay here," he ordered.

Ric must have flown up the stairs because in a flash he was coming down the hall. Ric didn't knock on the bathroom door, and he didn't hesitate to confront Dad while he was in the shower. It was quick.

"You like to hit women?" Ric popped off.

"Oh, turn around and go back home. This is none of your business," Dad quipped back.

All hell broke loose, and the fighting ensued. It sounded like a large round of ammunition going off.

"Agh!" Dad yelled, like the air had been sucked out of his lungs.

"Try it again," Ric dared him and then stomped off.

Back to the vent I went.

"It's taken care of. Call if you need me. He may have to go to the hospital," Ric told Lil as he left.

Dad was groaning on the other side of the wall.

Lil came back upstairs.

"That ends it. You don't lay a hand on me again, or next time it will be worse, and we're through," she screamed.

Dad just groaned.

Then there was struggling again, so I crept out and slid against the wall to peek around the corner. Lil was helping Dad up out of the tub. His nose was bleeding. He was holding his ribs and having a hard time breathing.

I stepped out and saw Lil throw a towel over Dad as he grabbed onto the sink.

"Go," he pointed, telling me to go back to bed. He didn't seem so scary at that moment, though.

"I'm going to have to take him to the hospital," Lil looked me in the eye. "He slipped in the shower and may have broken some ribs."

That he did. Several of them. It was gangster.

5

Just after Thanksgiving, Dad called me and Todd into the living room. We had caught on that it was his way of dropping big news on us.

"Sit, kids. I have something to tell you." He seemed excited and nervous at the same time.

We sat in our usual spots on the couch. Dad paced back and forth in front of us a few times and then exclaimed, "Lillie and I are getting married." He splayed his hands out as if saying *Wow, isn't that amazing?*

"Don't do it," I pleaded. "I can help take care of us. I'll learn whatever I have to. We can take care of ourselves."

"I'll help her," Todd begged.

"Now come on. Things have gotten a lot better. They're only going to get better."

Who did he think he was kidding? "Are you kidding? You see how she treats us?" I choked out.

"Don't get smart. Now clean yourself up, and go let Lillie know how happy you are for us."

Lil didn't get any happiness from me. My tear-stained face said it all. We weren't getting off the ride; we were stuck in hell.

*

Just shy of a year after Mom and Dad split, Dad married Lil at a church up the street in a quick ceremony with just us kids there.

It was a church I passed by almost every day and where I played in the parking lot, but I had never seen the inside. I had lain in the grass outside the church many times, awestruck by the color when the sun hit the stained glass windows. It was the first place since living in Pennsylvania that I'd felt the presence around me.

Seeing the windows up close from the inside, I took it all in but had no idea what the scenes depicted. Then there was the organ. It was even better than Lil's and had a stack of pipes behind it. And there was a chime room. The church rang the chimes hourly, and they had saved my butt many times getting back to Lil's on time.

Sitting in a pew, I picked up a Bible and fanned through it, wondering what it was all about.

Just then a man approached from behind. "Everybody all set?"

As I turned, he put out his hand.

"Hi, I'm Reverend Modisher. Who are you?" He had a warm, inviting smile.

Smiling back, I shook his hand. "I'm Traci."

"Yes, you are!" he exclaimed and scared me by his excitement.

I just stared at him.

"Do you know what you just told me?"

My expression told him no because not a word came out of my mouth.

"You not only told me your name but that you're a child of God."

I just stared at him.

He bent down to my level. "God is the Great I AM. When you said, 'I'm Traci,' you not only told me your name, but you told me you're a child of I AM, meaning God." He patted me on the head and walked down the aisle.

"You know, we have Bible study coming up. Your kids are welcome," Reverend Modisher told Lil after the ceremony.

Then we went to dinner as a "happy new family."

* * *

Scripture tells us in the Old Testament, "And God said to Moses, 'I AM WHO I AM.' And He said, "Thus you shall say to the children of Israel, 'I AM has sent me to you.'"[1]

In the New Testament, Jesus says to the Jews, "Very truly I tell you . . . before Abraham was born, I am!"[2]

In Hebrew, I AM is YHWH and means "the one who is always present."[3]

* * *

Lil had attended church by herself maybe a handful of times during the first year we lived with her. Some Sundays, she'd be dressed and gone before we got up. After she and Dad married, they started attending together more regularly.

"Would you kids like to go to church with us this Sunday?" Dad asked during dinner one night.

"Don't ask them, Steve. Tell them," Lil corrected.

"Lil would like us to attend church together Sunday as a family. Make sure you have decent clothes to wear," he told us.

*

The church was like something out of a movie—large, ornate, and beautiful. It was a Catholic church and very formal. I'd never seen anything like it and had no idea what was being said most of the time, but I didn't care. The people were up and down, kneeling and then standing. It was confusing. When it was over, I was full of questions.

"Why did Jesus have to die like that?"

"He died for us, for our sins," Lil responded.

"I don't understand."

"Me either," Todd added. "Why do they talk in another language?"

"You will learn. It takes time," Lil said. "We'll see about classes."

*

At school, a classmate named Matt came up to me one day.

"Hey, didn't I see you at church on Sunday?"

"Yeah."

"Didn't your parents just get married?" It was an odd question, but his mom was one of Lil's clients, so I assumed that's how he knew.

"Yeah."

"So they were divorced, right?"

"Yeah." I didn't understand his line of questioning. "Why?"

"Because you're not allowed to be divorced, stupid. It's a sin." He laughed at me. "Why do you guys even go to church?"

* * *

Life continued in Lil's house. Her nasty treatment escalated. She could find the smallest things to pick at such as the way my toothbrush was placed in the holder. There were times when she'd be nice and lift me up, and then the next chance she got, she'd kick me in the gut.

She caught me watching her practicing on the organ one day.

"Would you like to learn?" she asked.

"Can I?"

"We'll try it out. I'll see if my teacher can fit you in for a half hour after me." The piano teacher came to the house weekly.

After a couple of weeks, I loved it.

During dinner one night, Lil coldly told me, "Deloris heard you playing today and mentioned how good you're getting."

"Thank you."

Lil gave me an irritated snort with no added kudos for my progress. The next thing I knew, I wasn't taking lessons anymore. There was no explanation; they were just cut off.

*

Kristi lived a few houses down. We met when we were playing outside one day and quickly became road dogs. Whenever I was allowed to go out and play, I headed to her house.

"I don't want you playing with that girl down the street anymore," Lil announced after calling me in for supper one evening. "She's a bad influence."

"She's not!" I said.

"You're behaving like a lesbian. It looks bad, and I won't have it."

"We're not gay just because we're friends."

"It doesn't matter because you're not allowed to be around her anymore."

*

Once during my regular dental checkup, the dentist told Lil, "I recommend braces for Traci. If her teeth aren't corrected, they'll worsen as she ages and begin to chip."

Crooked teeth were a trait from the Serbian side of the family, and my incisors slanted somewhat backward.

"If that's something she wants to take care of, she can do it on her own when she's older," Lil snapped at him.

"Oh, all right," the dentist stammered as his eyebrows went up in surprise. He gave me a consoling pat on the shoulder as if to say *Sorry, I tried.*

Welcome to my world, dude, I thought.

* * *

Then the kicks started coming from the other side, too.

Mom and I had gotten into the habit of writing one another. Her letters were highlights during my life at Lil's house, something to look forward to. Then one particular letter opened up a whole new branch on our family tree.

"Hi, Honey. I'm writing with some news. I got married to a wonderful man," she started the letter. We had kept in regular contact by phone, but not once had she mentioned anyone special in her life. It hurt that she told me in a letter. Sadness hit me instantly. It felt like she was moving on without me and Todd, like we'd been replaced. I was crushed.

"Share my news with Toddy for me," she wrote. "Tommie will be coming to see you soon and tell you the rest. I love you kids."

It hit Todd like a brick, too. We both wondered what "the rest" meant.

* * *

A few months later, I ran into Tom's arms after not seeing him for almost two years. He had already graduated from high school. We went out to lunch so we could talk privately and catch up. It was like old times. Tom also sat down and talked to Dad. It was a conversation Todd and I weren't privy to. Tom was irritated afterward.

"What's wrong?" I asked Tom.

"I have a lot to tell you guys, stuff I wanted to talk about in person, not on the phone."

"Okay," Todd and I said as one.

Tom shook his head in disbelieving memory.

"He dragged Mom through the mud in the divorce. She tried to see you guys, but he . . . he used her health and . . . wouldn't let her talk to you guys to put pressure on her. He wouldn't even send her any pictures. He left her high and dry and cut off her health care. I took over her guardianship."

"What's that?" I asked.

"Mom needs care. She has to have someone help her manage life. She needed a guardian. I had to get insurance for us. That's what I've been doing, going to school and working. At least I was able to save enough to move out of Grandma's."

"What was your talk with Dad all about?" I asked.

"When I applied for my driver's license, I had to get a copy of my birth certificate, and I found out that Steve never adopted me."

"Adopted?" Todd and I said simultaneously, perplexed.

"Did you know he wasn't your dad?" Todd asked Tom, beating me to the question.

"Yeah, but I was always told that Steve adopted me. I thought that's why I had his last name. Once I got my birth certificate, Mom had to fess up. I had to go back to my birth name." There was hurt in his voice. "Life as I knew it was over because everything had to be changed—school enrollments, everything. So I confronted him and told him what a piece of crap I thought he was."

"What did he say?"

"He said he's sorry but there are things I don't know and wouldn't understand. Blah, blah . . . it's all excuses."

Next up was an even bigger surprise.

*

"When I graduated," Tom went on, "the local paper listed all our names in the paper. My real dad saw mine and showed up at the ceremony. That's when he reconnected with Mom."

Todd and I were in shock.

"What's he like?" I asked.

"He's cool. It's weird, but they seem happy. I'll get to know him, but I'm not sure how I feel yet. You know, he just left us when I was young. He never tried to keep in touch with me." Pain was in his voice.

"I can't believe we never knew all this," I returned.

"He lived right down the street from us when we moved to Cedarbrook. I used to see him when I rode my bike around. But then he was just gone one day." He raised his hands in the air to imply a poof.

"That's just crazy," I said incredulously.

"Hey, anyway, we need to get you guys to Ohio to see Mom. When we get back to the house, I'll talk to Lil and Steve about it."

It was strange hearing him call Dad by his name.

* * *

It had been two and a half years, and I was nervous to see Mom again. She and Tom's dad—Tom Sr.—came outside as we rolled up.

Mom looked good. She had put on some weight. Her long hair was down, her skin was clear, and she smiled with excitement. Todd and I ran out of the car and encircled her in a big hug.

"I'm so happy to see you guys," she exclaimed. "Let me look at you." We stepped back from her so she could give us the once over. "You've both grown so much!"

"You look good, happy," I told her. And she did, although she remained very fragile. Tom had cautioned us, and it was evident.

"I am happy, Honey. We have a lot of catching up to do. Oh, Honey, look at your hair." She ran her fingers through its shortness. It was still a sore subject.

"I know. I hate it, and I'm going to grow it back as soon as I'm out of that house."

"We'll get into that. Here, I want you to meet Tom," she turned and waved her hand in introduction. "Kids, this is Tom Sr., Tommie's dad." She said it like it was no big deal, just common knowledge.

"Hi, you two. It's so nice to meet you both," he said, holding out his hand. It was a weird, surreal meeting of a man now known as Tom's dad but not ours.

"Hi." I shook his hand. He seemed different, cooler, and hipper than Dad.

"Tom tells me you're into bikes."

"Yes, it's one of the first things I want when I'm on my own."

"Let me show you mine." He motioned for me to follow him. As soon as we rounded the corner, I saw a fully dressed Harley. He knew the way to my heart.

"Come. Come inside," Mom invited. Their apartment seemed small, but we settled in for our first meal together.

"So, did Tom tell you he has another brother?" Tom Sr. asked me and Todd.

"Nope," I responded quite frankly. "We haven't heard that one yet."

"Well, after your mother and I split, I did a lot of adventuring."

It was never lost on me how adults tried to spin on kids to make their lack of parenting sound better.

"I was married a second time, and we had Timmy. It didn't work out with his mother and me, though."

"Have you met Timmy?" I asked Tom.

"No, but I'd like to someday. It's all just . . . " he faded off, but I understood. We weren't in the same boat anymore, but we were both still rowing in the boat's broken pieces, just trying to hang on.

"Where's Tim now?" I asked Tom Sr.

"He lives in Arizona. He does something with the cops out there. We don't keep in touch too much, but he checks in every now and then."

"Traci, you talk a lot about getting out of Lil's," Mom said. "Do you have plans?"

"I'm saving money. I'm thinking about getting a paper route to save some more. I'll figure out how to get out of that house. But I know what I want to do when I graduate."

"Already?" Mom exclaimed.

"Geez," Tom said, "I'm still trying to figure that out for myself."

"Well, you don't live with Lil. That would make anyone figure it out quickly. I don't want to stay in that house a day longer than I have to."

"What goes on?" Mom asked.

With some input from Todd, we gave them the rundown. When we finally stopped talking, the table went silent for a few minutes.

"I'm sorry you kids are in that situation," Mom said sadly. "I thought you were being taken care of. What a thing, just over milk. You kids did drink a lot, but there's nothing wrong with that."

"I'll come and get you guys more regularly," Tom told us. "I'll get you out of there as much as possible. Whenever you need to talk, call me. If I have to come in the middle of the night, I will. At least Lil's good about letting you guys come and visit."

"Yeah, 'cuz it gets us out of the house and we're not costing her anything. We're just servants. I don't get what Dad sees in her. It's like he doesn't have the courage to go it on his own. Why did he marry her?" It felt good to vent.

"Hang in there for me, kid," Tom said. "So what are your future plans?"

* * *

When I got older, I asked Mom about when she and Tom Sr. met.

"We dated while I was at Andrews." Andrews was an all girls' school.

"When did you have Tom?"

"I was 19. Oh, it was a hard time then. I went to live in a facility for unwed, single, pregnant women."

"Did Tom Sr. know?"

"No. I kept him out of it because I didn't know what I was going to do yet."

Then she sobbed and said through tears, "I thought about giving Tommie up, but I couldn't. Eventually, I wrote Tom a letter. He told me he knew the baby was his. We got married, but it didn't last. He wasn't ready to be a dad. He was too interested in hanging out with his buddies."

6

Eventually, my relationship with Lil got better because I tried so hard to please her. Once she crowned me responsible, she started paying me to clean her salon. Dad went to bat for me on that one.

Then the paper route I'd been hoping for came through, and life got busy.

After school, chores came first, and then I'd pack up a saddle bag for each shoulder and hike up the hill to deliver papers. As I met and got to know my clientele, several of the families asked if I babysat, so I broke into that market. Lil helped me open my first savings account.

* * *

We attended church together most Sundays. But the novelty was broken by the ridicule I received from a group of kids at school. Todd felt it, too, by the stares and whispers from the pews in front of us. It was an uncomfortable, uninviting feeling. We felt like outcasts.

"What's with those kids a few rows up?" Lil asked me during the ride home. "Do you know them? Isn't one of them Dina's kid, Matt?"

"From school. They're kind of jerks."

"Why are they being jerks to you?"

"Don't know. Guess I don't fit in."

"That's ridiculous. Everyone fits in at church."

That statement bit her in the butt a few weeks later when she received a letter in the mail. Standing at the fridge for ice, I eavesdropped.

"Can you believe that?" There was hurt in her voice.

"Wait, what did it say?" Dad asked.

"We regret that because of your remarried statuses, church policy prohibits you from becoming members." She read on. "We welcome you to continue attending."

Talk about feeling like an outcast. I didn't understand church, but a couple of words I heard—*cursed* and *condemnation*—kept resonating. I felt them both and that our family was doomed.

* * *

"I don't want to go to church anymore," I announced during dinner a few nights later. "I'm not comfortable there, and neither is Todd."

"I understand that where I go to church may not be for you guys, but you have to go to church," Lil said. "So find one you like, and start going. There's the one up the street," she suggested.

Todd and I looked at one another and nodded. We both liked Reverend Modisher.

"We'll try that one," we both agreed.

* * *

As we got along better, talking to Lil grew easier at times. Just before heading out for a visit with Dad's side of the family, I shared my feelings about his family with her and was surprised by the compassion she returned.

"I get where you're coming from on that," she agreed. "After my mom . . . I got passed around a lot between family members. It was more what I could do for them."

*

During the visit with Dad's family and after dinner one evening, Aunt Mitza and Lil were chatting at the table while others were clearing it. I sat at the other end, thumbing through a magazine and listening to their conversation.

"How is it having two young kids in the house again?" my aunt asked Lil at one point.

"We've had our moments, but they're good kids. They've learned to do chores and have become good workers."

Kind words for servants. Geez, it was hard eavesdropping and keeping quiet.

"Oh, what do you have them doing?"

"All of it. Dishes, cleaning, vacuuming, laundry."

As they chatted on, my aunt's wheels were spinning. "You know, we've got things going on all the time here that would keep the kids busy," she slid into the conversation at one point.

My head snapped up from my pretend reading. Lil and I caught each other's eyes, and she winked quickly. Sitting back in the chair, I thought this should be good.

"Why don't you have the kids stay with me for a summer?" Aunt Mitza suggested.

"Have you ever had them before?" Lil asked.

"No, no. It was a different situation when they were with their mother."

"Different? How?"

Lil was good. Her inner gangster was coming out. She'd shoot me that look across the table every now and then. It was the same quick, steady gaze she gave me in the hallway when she was helping Dad with his broken ribs. It was a look that says, *Here's how you handle this.*

"Things were . . . the kids were not as responsible," my aunt explained.

Lil sat back in her chair, keeping her eyes steady on my aunt and letting an uncomfortable several seconds go by.

75

"I don't think so," Lil finally said. "You never cared to have them before, but now that you know they're more responsible, you . . . *no!*"

Aunt Mitza had no words. It was fantastic. She had revealed how hypocritical she was.

* * *

Todd and I gained a new perk by being deemed responsible. We could stay home alone when Dad and Lil went out, which was most Friday and Saturday nights. Those were the best times when we had the run of the place and didn't have to worry about getting any chores done.

We'd stay up late and watch whatever we wanted on TV, wrestle with each other, and eat whatever crap food we could get our hands on. We'd get our beds ready so when Dad and Lil got home, all we had to do was shut the TV off and quickly slip under the covers.

When they pulled up to the house, they were always hammered and loud. We'd quietly run to my bedroom to peek out the window and watch them put the car in the garage. It was always a comical situation.

The car was usually a bit crooked in the driveway. We'd giggle quietly and watch as one of them got out and lifted the garage door. Sometimes the two barn doors in front of it were also closed, and they'd have to open those by lifting the grounding pins and swinging each side open. It was quite a humorous task to accomplish while inebriated. Once they got the car in the garage, Todd would tiptoe across the hallway to his room.

* * *

We began attending church on our own. Todd and I stuck by each other on our venture up the hill into a new journey and sat in the balcony trying to take it all in. Without Lil there, we had the freedom to look around and not get flicked or told to sit still and keep our eyes forward.

As we watched other families interact, we realized it was nothing like our family situation. Children were with their parents, and families sat together and enjoyed one another.

As the service began, Todd and I went through the motions of what we saw around us. At least we understood what was being said this time around, sort of. The sermons were confusing because in our lives, there was all the bad stuff the Reverend spoke of—adultery, divorce, lying, stealing. Generations could be cursed, he told us, "yet he does not leave the guilty unpunished; he punishes the children and their children for the sin of the parents to the third and fourth generation."[1]

Leaving church that day, I believed our family was cursed, that God had abandoned us. I wondered who had finally tipped the scales and cast us out. Why did Dad and Lil even try? What was it all about?

As we walked outside, Reverend Modisher was shaking hands. On our approach, he grabbed my hand.

"I saw you two in the balcony. So glad you've come. Are you going to be with us for Bible study?"

"What is it exactly?" I asked.

"I teach the Bible to a class of kids your age. We learn about God, who He is, why He created us, and what He expects of us. We study how He sent us His Son, Jesus, that He was crucified for our sins, and that He gave us the Holy Spirit.

"I don't understand."

"Exactly," he said excitedly. "That's why you should come."

* * *

During another sermon, things about God really got muddled because he was teaching on a topic close to my heart. There were two sentences that burned into my brain and tore my heart.

"Animals don't go to heaven. They don't have a spirit."

"Do you really believe God wouldn't make a place for pets, Reverend?" I questioned him on the way out. As a devoted animal lover, the thought was heart-wrenching. The pets we had were part of my escape from life, one of my happy places. They were my family.

"I'm sorry to be the one to break it to you. You're bothered by it, I can see. But the Bible says there are no dogs in heaven." Then he held my hand. "That's just the way it is." It was like a parent telling a child Santa Claus isn't really real.

"Have you put any thought into Bible study? We start in two weeks. It would behoove you to come."

* * *

It was a 10-day study that Todd and I attended. The spiritual world hit home, and I wondered if it had anything to do with the presence I'd often felt.

But the symbolic language threw me—things like "bread of life" and why we're called sheep. The term *fear of the Lord* scared me since I didn't understand the true meaning. Worried about the curse, I felt ashamed. I wanted to run and hide. How do you turn to a Man by faith, someone referred to as Father, when the only example of a father left me feeling deserted and lost?

Jesus died for our sins but I didn't really grasp sin. Was that why Lil and Dad kept going to church, because they kept sinning? Was Dad afraid of God, too?

At the end of the Bible study course, the Reverend asked if I wanted to accept Jesus as my Savior. Lil told me it wasn't a choice. Still unsure of what it all meant but knowing it was important, I took time to think about it.

* * *

It had been a bad morning. Todd got in trouble and had to go to church with Dad and Lil. Things at home were a mess, and my mood was down. Sitting in my favorite spot in the church balcony, my thoughts drifted back to the sermon. Then I realized the presence was there. It had been for a while.

"You always show up when I feel the worst. Is that you, Lord?" I whispered.

Reverend Modisher was telling about Noah, how God set the rainbow in the sky.[2] I tried to picture the scene, a monstrous wooden boat stranded on a rocky mountainside somewhere and Noah and his sons nearby worshiping the Lord who had spared their lives. God's voice comes from the altar they built and tells them to go have babies and fill the earth. Then God makes promises and seals them with a rainbow in the cloudy sky after the storm.

Daydream mode kicked in, and I penned a poem on my church bulletin. Writing made me feel better. Sitting there in the pew with the comforting presence, I made the decision to accept Jesus as my Savior.

* * *

There came a time when I wanted to enter a writing contest at school and had several pieces to choose from. The one I selected was the short poem I had written at church. At dinner one night, I told Dad and Lil about the contest.

"I've never seen you write," Lil snorted back.

"Well, I like to, and maybe I have a piece good enough."

"Let me read it," she demanded.

"May I be excused for a second?"

"Go."

Lil read it twice and then looked over her glasses at me.

"You didn't write this!" she laughed and tossed the paper at me. "You don't know how to talk like that."

The poem won recognition in the A-Plus Section of the paper, and I never told my family or shared it with them. The credit goes to God.

* * *

Volunteering for a couple of local missions, I got to travel a bit. A group of us helped build parts of churches in low income areas in Kentucky.

During one particular outing, I discovered that Reverend Modisher wasn't an animal lover. It was obvious from his demeanor around them on the farm we were at. It was almost comical how put off he was when he got nosed by a cow. He wouldn't allow the dogs to come near him.

Taking a break one day, I spoke with an elder of the church about my confusion over God and His animals.

"I've always heard that God loves all His creation. Why wouldn't He make a place for animals?" I asked.

"What makes you think that?"

"Reverend's teaching just a while back."

"Oh," she paused in thought. "As with any teacher, religious instructors have their own interpretations and opinions when it comes to scripture."

"What do you mean?"

"Because of the things we go through, our life experiences, and how we learn, we all see things differently."

* * *

Reverend had been a harsh believer. He taught the love of God but taught a lot about God's anger, that He punishes and is extremely strict. He was very Old Testament, which I define as God's war against sin before sending the Lamb.

Had I held on long enough as a teen, learned to reference and study the Bible myself, it would have led me to understand the curse and given me the key to remove it.

The elder's advice was misleading. Just because we all go through stuff doesn't mean that God's Word changes accordingly. God's Word is God's Word.[3]

As a pet lover, I ask through prayer to see them again and be with them in heaven. God loves what we love. We were made in His image.[4]

God communicates with animals. How else could Noah have gotten all of them to the ark and then inside?[5] The Lord fed Elijah with ravens.[6] He knows every sparrow.[7] Balaam and the donkey![8] There's so much in that story.

God enjoys animals.[9] He created and designed them in different varieties, appointed their roles, and provides for them just as He does us. Animals display the Lord's sovereignty.[10]

It would have all sunk in had I just continued studying the Bible and asked the Lord to open my eyes.[11]

But Reverend retired, and I was left feeling numb. Survivor mode kicked in strong as life at home intensified. Church life became more of a place for socializing, and with all the drama that came with it, I stopped attending.

* * *

Just before my 16th birthday, Lil got new carpet in her dining room. After I helped Dad push a large china hutch back in place, he stepped back and started rubbing his chest up by his shoulder.

"My arm feels funny." He suddenly turned pale.

"You okay, Dad?"

"Not sure. I'm going to sit down outside for a minute."

It was as if an illness had taken over.

He stepped outside the dining room door, sat down on the step, and lit a cigarette. He took a drag or two, put it out, and then just sat there. I went into the kitchen to do some dishes.

A couple of minutes later, he came in, still rubbing the area he'd been complaining about.

"I'm going to lie down for a bit. Will you check on me in a few minutes?"

"Yes," and I meant it because Dad was even pastier looking and had beads of sweat across his forehead.

A couple minutes later, it wasn't good.

"My arm is tingling. Will you go get Lil?"

Lil was working on a client and heard me approach at the back door of the salon. It was one of the few times I remembered to stop at the doorway. She didn't like it when we talked to her in front of clients.

She turned, and I waved her to the back.

"Dad's having a stroke or something."

She flew up the stairs, and I followed. As soon as she looked at Dad, I knew it was bad. We helped him up and got him out to the car. She sped off, leaving her client sitting in the chair.

* * *

Dad was in the hospital when my birthday rolled around. He survived the heart attack. He quit smoking immediately, cold turkey, and never smoked again.

Since I was now old enough to work, I gave up my paper route and got a job as a waitress. The restaurant was across town, so when Dad was in the hospital, I asked him to teach me how to drive when he got out. Since he was in the hospital, I knew he'd be soft on me.

He took me out driving once. When Lil found out, she threw a fit and put a stop to it.

"No, Steve," she told Dad right in front of me. "We're not doing this. It's going to end up costing us."

* * *

Before leaving for Jamestown that last Christmas when Mom and Dad separated, Mom had pulled me into one of Grandma's bathrooms. She was butt naked and running the water to fill the tub.

"Honey, I don't know when I'm going to get to see you again, and I want to make sure you're prepared when you get your period," she told me in that strange speech she'd get.

Paying attention, I just stood there scared.

"Now, when it shows up, you might get some cramping."

She turned and took something off the sink.

"This is a pad. It goes in your underwear, like this." And she demonstrated.

"This is a tampon, and it goes in your vagina like this." Could've done without that demonstration, but I hung in there.

"Do you understand, Honey? I love you and just want you to be prepared."

* * *

Headaches began plaguing me, and I was in a funk. Afraid of being "sick like Mom," I rarely spoke up about not feeling well. It was a fear I carried for a long time until I finally learned about her illness.

The source of what was ailing me reared its head in the form of womanhood. Thankfully, what Mom had taught me kicked in. In her failing mental state, she had cared enough to teach me something that my stepmother didn't want to be bothered with.

When Lil came in from shopping with her sister who was visiting from New Jersey, they saw me at the basin in the basement.

"What are you doing?" Lil stopped in the doorway.

"Washing out my underwear. My period started."

She looked over my shoulder.

"Make sure you get it all out."

Then she turned and walked upstairs. Not another word was said about it.

* * *

Almost the minute I started high school, Lil rode my butt about what I was going to do after I graduated.

"If you're planning on going to community college and want to continue living here, you're paying rent," she told me during my junior year.

"I don't exactly know what I'm doing yet, but I guarantee I won't be living here."

She threw a haymaker at me. When I blocked it with my forearm, shock overcame her face. The memory of it gives me pleasure to this day.

*

Unbeknownst to her and Dad, I had been thinking a lot about what I was going to do. Staring out the windows at school, I'd planned my escape and thought about it every day until I finally made the decision to enlist. The commercials for the Marine Corps really got to me, especially the one when an ordinary man was transformed into a proud, sword-carrying, strong Marine. Dad had nurtured my love for planes, and I wanted to work on them.

I approached him about it one day, and I thought he'd be thrilled.

"Hey, Dad. I decided to join the Corps. Will you sign for me so I can enlist early?"

His eyes went wide, and his head snapped back a little.

"No, absolutely not. If you want to go into the service, you can go in the Navy. I'm not giving you permission to join the Marines."

So I waited until I was 17. I actually did test for the Navy, scoring high in mechanical and electrical skills, but the recruiter blew it because he kept insisting I go into administration. Walking out of his office, I enlisted in the Marine Corps with a guaranteed contract to the West Coast.

*

A few weeks later, mustering up the courage to tell Dad, I approached him one night in the kitchen while he was cooking dinner.

"Can I talk to you a sec?"

"Yeah." But he didn't look at me. He was standing at the sink cleaning chicken.

"I tested for the military and did well for avionics. I joined the Marines."

He turned and looked at me and then went back to the chicken. I waited as he washed his hands and then threw them into the air, exasperated, slamming his palms down on the edge of the counter.

"I tried. It's up to you."

He was pissed.

*

A few nights later, Lil went bowling, and it was just the three of us. Dad was drunk and in a foul mood. Still mad at me for signing up, he was looking for a fight that night.

"You're going to get eaten alive in the Marines. When you come home with your tail between your legs, I'll be the first one to say I told you so." The tone in his voice was taunting, I didn't take the bait.

But Todd did.

"She'll do great. I'm thinking about enlisting, too, when I graduate."

Todd was sitting across the kitchen table from Dad, and I was at the sink a few feet away. As I turned to look at Todd, Dad shot up with so much force that he bashed his chair against the wall, making a big dent.

Putting some more distance between me and Dad, I stepped back quickly thinking he was coming after me. At the same time, Todd jumped up from his chair.

Dad flew around the table toward him. Todd turned and ran. I stood there for a couple of seconds, panicked, and then went after them.

By the time I reached the doorway of my brother's room, Dad had caught up to him and was wailing on him. Todd was trying to tuck himself in a ball to ward off the blows.

As soon as I saw the scene, I jumped on Dad's back. He threw me off, sailing me into the wall, just missing the dresser. As I stood up, Dad whipped around and looked at me with animal in his eyes.

Crap! I thought. *He's between me and the door.*

He tried to dive for me. Jumping over him and ricocheting off the bed, I ran—right out the dining room door in my bare feet into the rainy night. At Kristi's, I called Debbie, a friend from school who lived across town. Debbie and her mom came and got me.

*

Lil called the next morning.

"What on earth happened?"

Relaying the story, I added, "I'm not coming back."

"Don't say that. Let's let things cool down. I'll call you in a little while."

Refusing to go home, I stayed with Debbie and her mom for about a week. Lil called every day trying to get me to go back. She finally showed up and wouldn't leave until I went with her.

"Your Dad's really sorry. This was a wake-up call for him."

Grudgingly, I went back, and we never discussed it again.

"What went on after I left?" I asked Todd.

"He didn't know what to do. By the time he reached the door, you were gone. Where'd you go?"

"Kristi's, and then I called Debbie. Did he leave you alone after that?"

"Yeah. That was crazy."

Eight months to go until graduation.

7

It was the summer of 1984. Lil threw a barbecue for my graduation celebration, and I could invite whoever I wanted, even Kristi. I also invited Mark and Dorothy, a young couple from my former paper route. The three of us initially bonded through our love of animals. When I delivered their paper, I'd stop and play with their German Shepherd, Reba. Eventually, we struck up a conversation and got to know each other.

We became friends and hung out. Over time, we shared about our respective family lives. They both had their own parental issues growing up, and we just seemed to have a connection. They knew I had enlisted and offered to take me into their home until I left. I jumped at the chance.

* * *

About a month after the barbecue, it was time. After supper one night, I grabbed an opportunity to approach Dad, Lil, and Todd who were relaxing in the living room.

"Can I talk to you guys about something?"

"Go ahead," Dad answered.

"I'd like to move out. The opportunity for a place to stay came up, so I'm letting you know."

"Where do you think you're going to go?" Lil asked. "This is the first we've heard of it."

"I told you before that I planned to leave after I graduated."

"Why?" Dad asked.

Poor Todd just sat there. He knew it was coming. I had only hung on that long for him.

"I'm sick of watching you drink yourselves to sleep every night. I'm tired of the arguing and games, and it's time for me to go." My voice shook hard.

"Where are you going?" Dad asked.

"Mark and Dorothy offered their house until I leave in January."

"Who are they?" Lil asked.

"The couple with the kids that you met at the barbecue."

"They're bad news," Dad said.

"You don't even know them."

"You're just trading your unhappiness for a different kind of trouble," Dad said. "Go to your room and think about it."

Doing just that, I packed a small bag and then quietly slipped out the dining room door. Sobbing, I walked past the church as I prayed for Todd who I had left behind in hell.

*

I called the next day, and Lil picked up. "Can I please talk to Dad?"

Her end of the phone slammed hard onto the table. "Steve," she yelled. "She's on the phone."

"Tell her to hang on. I'll run upstairs," Dad said.

"I'm not telling her anything," Lil snapped.

Dad picked up the other line.

"There's just no telling you anything, huh? You okay?" Dad said sadly.

Lil loudly hung up on her end.

"Yeah. Is it okay if I stop by to pick up some of my stuff?"

"I'm here. See you when you get here."

*

When I walked back down the hill that afternoon, Dad was mowing the lawn. He saw me coming and stopped to talk.

"I didn't want you to leave home like this."

"This was never home, and I can't live like this anymore, Dad. I'm done."

"You've got a plan?" His eyes welled up.

"For now, at least until I leave."

"Well, Lil was mad," he said, looking to the ground. "I tried to stop her." He kicked a clump of grass in frustration and then looked at me again. "She packed up your stuff. It's on the front patio."

He walked with me. Sure enough, everything of mine was in boxes.

"I hate this," Dad said. We just stood there for a few seconds.

"I'll take what I can carry. Can I come right back for the rest with Mark and Dorothy?"

"Get it done," he said walking off. "I'll keep Lil occupied."

* * *

Todd stopped by to see me a few days later.

"I miss you," he told me and gave me a big hug.

"Miss you, too, and I hated leaving you. You have to hang in there. Your day will come. I'm always here for you."

"I know."

"You can come and see me anytime," I told him.

"Yeah, but I have to be careful 'cuz Lil banned me."

"Whatever. Anytime, okay?"

*

On my birthday, Dad sent Todd to deliver a card. He had written this short note inside. "Now that you're grown and gone, I'd like to buy you your first legal drink." He signed it "Dad" and enclosed 20 bucks. It gave me hope that we might be able to repair our relationship one day.

"He quit drinking," Todd said. "Cold turkey."

"Really?"

"Yep."

"Because of what I said?"

"Don't know, but I think so. He says he's done."

"What's that like?"

"So far, so good. He seems fine with it."

"Did Lil quit?"

"No. He still takes drinks to her."

I celebrated my birthday with friends. Then grown-up life hit, and things went sideways.

* * *

My first experiences with "clubbing" were with Dorothy. She loved to dance and invited me along, so I took her up on it. About the second or third time we went out, she asked me as we sat at a table chatting, "Are you getting excited to leave?"

"You know it. Ready to get out of Jamestown."

"You're lucky you get to make the escape."

"Yeah, but you and Mark are happy. You guys like it here and have a great relationship. Hope I can find somebody someday."

"It's not all it's cracked up to be," she said sadly.

"What do you mean?"

"I've been unhappy for a long time."

Never sensing anything wrong between the two of them, I was shocked. They seemed to enjoy each other and did things together, and they were great parents.

"What are you going to do?" I asked.

"Don't know, but I don't want to live life unhappy, so I'm going to make myself happy." Then she shut down the conversation and wanted to party.

Within minutes, a man walked into the bar and waved to us from across the room. As he headed our way, Dorothy grabbed my arm and pulled me over to her so I could hear what she wanted to tell me over the sound of the music.

"He's a coworker I'm interested in. I've been following him to see where he goes, hoping to run into him."

He approached our table, and Dorothy morphed into a ho-bag.

So this is how an affair begins, I thought. Instantly bummed to be in the middle of a situation, I quietly stepped back from her scene.

Dorothy started going out a lot by herself. Her evening attire became provocative—short, tight dresses and heels. Even the way she dressed for work changed from her usual jeans and shirts to dresses and heels.

One night after the kids went to bed and Dorothy went out, Mark struck up a conversation with me as we were doing the dinner dishes.

"I'm starting to wonder what's going on with her," he told me with annoyance in his voice. "Do you know anything?"

"No." It was a lie. Crap!

"Well, I have some suspicions." He ticked off a few names and then asked, "Do you know any of them?"

"No." That was the truth.

"Dorothy tells me the names of people she's going out with all the time. She says they're friends from work." Then he went on a rant. "Look at the way she's starting to dress. If she's going out with the girls, what's she doing dressing like that?"

Feeling for him, I ended up telling him what I knew and made him promise he wouldn't tell Dorothy or confront her until I was gone. I felt stuck again and didn't know how to get unstuck.

* * *

Thanksgiving came. Mark and Dorothy spent the day with her family.

Hanging out with their dog, I cried the day away, miserable and alone. I got angry and cried some more, missing my family. The comfort zone of Mark and Dorothy was gone. The tension in the house became thick. I felt betrayed by them, too, that it was wrong to invite me into their house when they were having issues.

The day felt like a year. Several times I opened the mirror cabinet in the bathroom and stared at the pill bottles thinking that death would be better than the pressing loneliness.

It was a very dark day, and I reached out in prayer for the first time since leaving the church.

"Are you there, God? 'Cuz I don't know what to do."

"Get up," my mind urged.

Lifting my head from my knees and letting my tears subside, I heard my favorite place calling. I picked myself up, went outside, and took Reba for a walk.

* * *

The summer of my 16th birthday after Dad had recovered from his heart attack, we all took a road trip to Colorado to visit Mary Jane and Jimmy, Lil's kids. Mary Jane was married, had two kids, and had her own clothing store. Jimmy was working in auto sales and still rooming with his friend Terry.

Aside from the car ride, the trip was great. I spent a lot of time hanging out at Jimmy's.

Terry and I hit it off and spent time together. He invited me to a Fourth of July celebration. Accepting shyly, I became instantly self-conscious.

Terry was partially deaf, wore hearing aids, and could read lips, so he would focus intensely on my face while communicating. Uncomfortably aware of his attraction for me, it was hard not to return it because it was there.

With Dad's permission, Terry picked me up. It was my first date. With no idea what to expect or what to say, I was nervous. Terry made it easy. He loved to talk and ask questions. We laughed, cracked jokes, and flirted, though I really didn't know how.

Terry pulled into a park and asked me to wait so he could open my door. Then we walked back to the trunk. He pulled out a picnic basket, a cooler, and a blanket. Taking me by the hand, he led the way.

It was still early, so the park wasn't crowded yet. Picking out a spot, we settled in. Terry had stopped at a deli he'd been bragging about. He pulled out a fat sub for us to share along with chips and drinks.

"Do you know what you're doing yet after you graduate?" he asked before digging into his half of the sub. I was still trying to figure out how to attack mine without coming out of it a mess. I was glad for the interruption.

"Yeah, actually. I'm going into the service."

He looked at me with surprise.

"That's so great. I'm excited for you. I wanted to, but my hearing." He threw his hands into the air as if to say, *What are you gonna do?* Then he asked, "What do you want to do?" He took another bite.

"Work on planes."

Finding the sweet spot on my sandwich, I went in for the kill. Terry's bragging was on point because the sub was outstanding.

"Have you hit your parents with it?"

"Dad. I got shot down. He wants me to join the Navy."

"What do you want?"

"Marines."

"Marines! Go on. Really?"

With my mouth full, I nodded my head yes.

"Tough girl, huh? Why the Marines?"

"I just . . . always liked the commercials. The pride and camaraderie—the few, the proud," I smiled teasingly.

"Boy, are they in trouble," he laughed.

After we were done eating, we laid down on the blanket and shared about our families, dreams, fears, and hobbies.

"You dating anyone back home?" he asked.

"Are you kidding? You know what my household's like. I'm

sure you've heard stories from Jimmy. Would you bring someone into that?"

"Sorry it's like that. Jim says it's pretty rough."

He reached for me, taking my arm and pulling me hand over hand to lay my head on his chest. In his arms, listening to his heartbeat, I thought this is what it's like to be with someone and not be in fear for what might be coming next. There was no snide remark, hiss of superiority, or a put-down. It was unnatural but serene. I'd never been with anyone and shared silence in such a way.

"Let's roll. I have a surprise for you," Terry said after lying there for a while.

We packed up and took off. A few minutes later, we were pulling into the driveway of someone's house. There was a party going on.

"That's not what we're here for. Come on, let's go claim our spot," he said.

Grabbing my hand, he led me to a back house where we climbed a staircase up to the roof. The sky opened up above the trees over the park we had just left. It was an incredible view. Terry waved his arm in ta-da fashion and gave me a big smile.

Some friends of his greeted us as we selected a seat for the best fireworks show I'd ever seen. It was perfect timing because the sun was dipping low. Terry scooted me close and put his arm around me.

"The best spot in the place for a beautiful woman," he leaned over and whispered.

I turned to look at him. He tipped his head, and we kissed.

* * *

Terry and I kept in touch. For the Christmas holiday, he was in town visiting family. We tried to make plans to see each other, but it wasn't working because I was leaving for Ohio. Tom arrived, and then Terry showed up.

"Hi," I greeted Terry with a hug. "This is a surprise. I didn't think we were going to get to see each other."

"I wanted to surprise you," he said. Lifting me off my feet, he squeezed me and held me. "I know you're headed out, but I wanted to give you something." He set me back down.

"Terry, this is Tom, my older brother."

"Sorry to drop by unexpected, man." Terry offered Tom his hand, and they shook. "I didn't want to miss her before she takes off."

"No problem. Nice to meet you, Terry."

Tom shot me a sly look as if to say, *This is something you haven't shared.*

"So, I wanted to send you off with something to remember me by."

Terry turned to me, stepped back, lowered his head, and took off his necklace, a beautiful silver cross he always wore. He reached around my neck and clasped it on.

"To keep you safe in everything you do."

Then he gently lifted my chin, and . . . it was an intimate kiss. My legs were going to give out.

"Have a great visit with your family. Kick ass in boot. I'll see you on the other side," Terry told me with a smile.

"Thank you—for the cross, for everything."

"Take care of yourself, and stay safe."

His goodbye kiss was less mushy, and then he was gone.

Not knowing how to handle his attention, I was instantly embarrassed, especially in front of Tom. Terry's interest was intense, more than I was ready for. When we talked by phone, he often spoke about future things together. Countering his statements with *I don't knows* and *we'll sees* and reminding him I was leaving for the military didn't seem to sink in, and it was off-putting.

Tom busted my chops over that encounter for the first half of the trip.

"Where'd you meet him?"

After telling him the story, I asked, "How do you get the point across that you're not interested in moving forward?"

"Well, you're leaving, right?"

"Yeah."

"Don't worry about it then. You're out of here."

Sitting back in the seat, I relaxed. He was right. It felt good to be alone with Tom and just talk.

Tom had gotten engaged right around the time I graduated. Nancy came with him to the barbecue. They had already bought a house and seemed amazingly happy.

As we neared their place, I surveyed the area—beautiful, woodsy, lots of farms and space. It was a dismal day, though, with a mixture of clouds stacked in billowy layers. One cluster resembled an angry Michelin Man with a snarled face of changing gray movement. Imagining the scene in color, I pictured the bare trees in full bloom on a clear, early summer day. It would be spectacular.

We were on a gravel road made smooth by snow and ice. It was a slow go to avoid sliding off into one of the drainage ditches on either side.

"Here we are," Tom pointed off to his left.

Tipping my head to look up a small hill, I saw their house nestled at the top and surrounded by snow banks. Smoke was rising from the chimney and settling in the low-lying clouds. As soon as I took in their brown ranch style home, it brought to mind our childhood house in State College.

Tom turned and went up the long incline.

"How's this to shovel?" I laughed.

"Are you kidding? I bought a plow."

*

It was an amazing time spent with family. Everyone was supportive of my decision to enlist. There was no backlash or negative talk—only encouragement. I welcomed the encouragement since that wasn't the type of support I got in Jamestown. It boosted my morale because although ready, I was nervous.

It was also time spent with a new friend. Nancy introduced me to her brother, Ted, who was home from college for the holidays. We had a lot in common and spent time together. After Christmas, he asked me out to a New Year's Eve party.

Ted liked to dance, so we tore it up and had a blast. When the midnight hour approached, everyone grabbed a glass for a toast. Ted and I got ready as the countdown began. As midnight struck, we raised our glasses, and then the horns blew and the noisemakers went nuts.

Reaching up to right the falling party hat on Ted's head, he leaned forward, and we kissed, the hat forgotten.

As the night wore on, there was more drinking, and Ted got falling down drunk. He literally fell down a flight of stairs. Like the scarecrow from Oz, he flailed down the steps trying to stay upright, but by the time he reached the bottom, he was in a crumpled heap. Then he popped right back up, standing like it was an act he'd been doing all along. Funny, but not funny. It was sobering to watch and reflect on what my home life had been like due to alcohol. An overwhelming feeling of escape hit me, so I called Nancy to pick us up.

"I'm sorry for last night," Ted apologized the next day. "I took it too far and didn't mean to scare you."

We hung out for the last couple of days of vacation and stayed in touch for a while afterward. He had a good head on his shoulders and vision for the future, and I valued our conversations and the advice he gave me about going for my dreams. Ted kept a special place in my heart for a long time as the type of man for my future.

But the bottom would have to hit before I figured that out.

* * *

Back in Jamestown, it was time to pack and go.

Mark and Dorothy drove me to MEPS, the Military Entrance Processing Station, in Buffalo. There was very little communication between us on the drive there. Their relationship was still deteriorating. My thoughts were on what lay ahead.

They saw me off with a hug from each of them, and then Dorothy handed me a small box.

"We wanted you to have something to remember us by."

In the box was a small sapphire ring, my favorite stone.

"Will you keep this safe for me with the other stuff until I get back?" I asked, teary-eyed.

We said our goodbyes, and then I walked into the building without looking back. After reporting in and getting a final physical, I was loaded down with a ton of paperwork to complete and sign.

All recruits stayed overnight in a hotel. It was our last night of civilian living, but there was definitely no celebrating. Eventually, I settled in for a restless night of sleep, awaiting the bus ride to Parris Island.

We were loaded up around 9:00 a.m. and ready for a long ride, approximately 14 hours. The first couple hours of the trip, there were a lot of conversations going on between different groups who were filled with anticipation. But everyone eventually settled in, and it grew quiet.

Attempting to sleep but just dozing off here and there, I kept waking up to see how far we'd gotten. A couple hours before we reached the base, the bus started to buzz again. But during the last hour, it was restrained.

8

Around midnight, we drove through the front gate and traveled on a bit to an auditorium. The first drill instructor (DI) made his entrance.

"Listen up," he boomed. "You're going to depart the bus and then line up single file outside. Do it now!"

We were herded into the auditorium for receiving and then seated in the bleachers while DIs took turns bellowing out instructions for what we were to do next.

"Listen up. You're going to line up in groups alphabetically for roll call."

Stations were set up where we received uniforms, boots, and everything else that went with entering military life. Our civilian clothes were taken away, and we cammied up.

When we had accomplished all that, we lined up outside again. It was after 2:00 a.m. We took the sloppiest march of our service careers to the barracks because we didn't know what we were doing, and we were all so tired we could barely see straight.

We were assigned bunks and footlockers.

"Listen up. Attention," screamed a DI. "Grab your personal things and shower. Quickly! I want you all in your racks in 10."

Modesty went out the window, and I took the fastest shower of my life. Exhausted and ready to pass out, my eyes shut before my head hit the pillow.

"Lights out, recruits. Get some rest. You're going to need it."

* * *

A couple of hours later, calamity struck loudly as aluminum garbage cans crashed down the aisles and DIs bashed the lids of the cans together like cymbals.

"Line up!"

Everyone jumped out of the rack. But as the green wool socks I'd slept in hit the glossy, freshly waxed deck, my feet came right out from under me. It was like ice, but there was no snow bank around to catch me. The smack of my body hitting the floor was hard and raw.

Recruits in the vicinity started cracking up. I did, too, to keep from crying. But it was funny.

Immediately, a short, petite Puerto Rican DI came over and laid into us as I was still trying to pick myself up.

"Ah, we have a bunch of funny girls, you unsat bunch of losers. Line up!"

Staff Sergeant Malone hopped up on my footlocker so we were eye-to-eye. She tore me a new one in a mixture of Spanish and English and then completed her rant by spitting in my face. "Recruit, what is your name?"

The last piece of advice from my recruiter rang in my ears. *Fly under the radar, and keep your head low. Don't bring attention to yourself so you don't get called out.*

Anonymous went out the window, and that DI was on my butt pretty much all of boot camp.

* * *

Largely due to Lil's conditioning, the mind games the DIs played weren't that bad. Marching was my favorite, especially drilling with rifles. It was an amazing feeling when the entire platoon was in step, the sound of our collective boots hitting the ground while cadence was called.

In classes, we were taught Marine Corps history, and we studied terrorism and homeland security. Then came combat training, weapons training, and lifesaving skills such as CPR.

Running was rough, and I knew I was going to have to train hard to keep up.

Midway through boot camp, a letter from Dad arrived.

"I hope you're hanging in there. I'm proud of you," he wrote. "Please come home before you head to your first duty station." The end of his letter choked me up. "I miss seeing you, and it's sad when I look at your picture in my dressing room. I'll write you again soon and look forward to hearing from you. Love, Dad."

It was the first time since childhood that he had told me he loved me, and it meant the world. Looking forward to seeing him and Todd put extra pep in my step for the remainder of training.

* * *

The crucible was the most brutal. It was a five-mile run in combat boots with a 50-pound pack and a rifle—the most exhausting and physically demanding experience of my life. After that came field and rifle training and then repelling the wall and free repelling from a tower. We crawled through dirt and mud while DIs shot tracer bullets overhead during a night infiltration course. It was scary but kind of fun.

Next came the gas chamber, which was not enjoyable at all. Like everything in boot camp, it was one of those trials that tests mental capability, physical stamina, breathing, and self-control all at the same time.

We entered the chamber in groups of 15 along with a handful of DIs. A couple of groups went through before my time was up. I was scared out of my mind. -

As others came out, I tried to pay attention to who had lost their cool and who hadn't. It wasn't hard to tell. Those who had lost it were hacking and coughing, snotting all over themselves and trying not to touch their stinging eyes. The people who hadn't lost their cool were struggling to catch their breath but were in better shape. Better shape was the way to go.

Time was up. Our group was instructed to form a circle around a small pile of crystals arranged in something like a mini fire pit. For about 10 minutes, we did exercises—sit ups, jumping jacks, and more.

The physical side of it helped take my mind off what we were about to do. But that's not what it's meant for. The DIs wanted us to sweat so our pores were open for the experience of the tear gas.

When it was time for the crystals to be lit, all but two DIs left the chamber to watch from the outside. The two remaining were fully suited up, and one lit the pile.

We stood with our masks at our feet trying to control our breathing and our fear. We were instructed to close our eyes as soon as the smell of the gas hit the air. We collectively stopped breathing and held our breath until we were given the don and clear.

My head was bowed as the gas began to sting my skin. My eyes were clenched tightly. Those who panicked were the first to start choking. With that going on around me, my concentration broke.

Slipping, needing to breathe, I tried to figure out how to best take a breath, not wanting to hold it too long and then suck in a big lungful. With a baby sip, I could taste the gas and started to do those jerky small coughs that come when you try to hold your breath again and try not to panic. I thought I was going to lose it, and then the don and clear came.

Dropping down to a knee, feeling around for the mask, and fumbling with the straps for a few seconds, I finally got it situated correctly, put it over my face, and then cleared and sealed it.

* * *

After completing the last phase with swimming, sharpening drill skills, and final testing, graduation day grew close. It was an amazing sense of accomplishment.

The afternoon and evening before graduation, recruits were given leave to enjoy and spend time with friends and family. It was just me, so I hung out with friends. As we were walking through the PX, suddenly there was Terry walking toward me.

So much for getting out of Dodge. Seeing Terry didn't feel like running into a friend. Instead, it felt overbearing. I couldn't return the smile he greeted me with.

"Who's that?" one of the girls asked.

"Could you guys give me a sec?" I answered and headed toward Terry.

"I wanted to surprise you," he grinned.

"You should've let me know you were thinking about coming." It was a stale comment.

"Then it wouldn't have been a surprise." He leaned in for a kiss, but I put my hand on his chest, stopping him.

"You're not surprised?" His smile faded.

"It doesn't feel like a surprise. It feels . . . invasive."

His beaming welcome turned into confusion, and I had to look away.

"You don't want me here?"

Looking down, I didn't answer.

Terry gently lifted my chin so we were eye-to-eye. "Do you want me to go?"

It was how I felt, but couldn't get the words out. Lifting my chin off his finger, I nodded yes, and the crushed look that overcame him shamed me. He turned and walked away.

"What was that all about?" the same girl asked as they gathered around me.

"My first battle."

* * *

The visit with Dad and Todd went great. Sober Dad was relaxed and kicked back. His whole demeanor had been revamped. He spoke kindly and gave advice in a caring way, not just his way. He had a new lease on laughter.

Todd was doing well, still fighting the fight, but had planned his way out. With four years to go, he was determined to enlist.

Lil was the same. The first thing she said as she pointed at my legs was, "Jesus Christ, you look like a goddamn man!"

It was good to see Mark and Dorothy, but it felt great to be out of there. They were better but struggling. An element of drama was added—Dorothy was pregnant as a surrogate for her sister. It was an amazing gift to give someone, but with their issues, it just added to the chaos that was them.

* * *

A couple of weeks later, I touched down in Memphis and took a bus to the naval base in Millington to learn Identification Friend or Foe (IFF),[1] an identification system that enables an aircraft to identify another aircraft as friendly or not. School was fun—trying at times but a great learning experience. It was my first taste of what life would be like. It was still a controlled environment but not like boot camp.

Students lived in barracks, and we all had chores to do, regular inspections to go through, group runs, you name it. There were no DIs. Instead, we had a barracks manager. Each student took turns nightly as the duty manager after the barracks manager went home in the evenings.

* * *

Tennessee reminded me a lot of Pennsylvania with its green, plush forests. On an early spring evening, I headed out, not really knowing what to do, so a walk sounded great. I was still running off the high of the visit with Dad and Todd, and it felt good to be following my dream, making it happen.

Lying down in the grass at a park, admiring the stars, I thought about God and wondered if He was there.

"I made it, Lord. I got up off the floor and kept going."

His glory was all around me, and it was serene. And that's where I should've stayed.

My thoughts were interrupted by a group of people laughing and joking as they went by.

"Dude, your score was crap."

"I thought you were going down with the ball the last time you were up. You should've lightened it a couple pounds."

They were talking about bowling. It reminded me of Dad, so I got up and went to investigate.

I went the way they had come, down a couple of blocks to an intersection and then to the left and up another block where there was a bright red bowling pin in the sky. Inside, the sounds and smells brought memories of Dad laughing and joking with his buddies, sitting on a lane bench with a cigarette hanging out of his mouth. Watching as a few people chastised one another over their throwing forms, someone stepped up beside me.

"Hey, I know you."

Turning, I greeted a fellow Marine.

"Hi, I'm Traci. I've seen you at school."

"Right. Gino." He gave me a big smile, and we shook hands. "You here by yourself?"

"Yeah, just checking it out."

"Me too. Wanna bowl together?"

He seemed nice, paid for us both, and bought me a drink. After selecting a lane and changing shoes, we both got up to pick out a ball.

"So, what made you join?" he asked.

"Just always wanted to. My dad was in the Navy, talked about planes a lot. It got to me."

"Dads have a way of doing that." He had a nice smile, radiantly white against the dark tone of his skin. "Ready to get your butt kicked?" He slapped me teasingly on the arm.

We started out bowling, two people acquainted from school, talking and getting to know one another. We were having fun, but the drinks were flowing way too much, and at some point, the flirting began. By the time we tired, we had played a handful of matches. While we were changing back into our shoes, Gino leaned over, and we kissed.

"Let's get out of here," he said.

Leading me by the hand, he walked us out together into the cool night air. It was a bit crisp, and I wished I'd brought a jacket, but I hadn't planned on being out so late.

"Let's walk," I told him. "I'm pretty buzzed."

A short distance later, we rounded a corner to a dimly lit, tree-lined area before the forest. Gino took my hand.

"Come with me."

He led me over to a large tree and pulled me to him, kissing me as he backed me up against the tree where we continued making out. Then we began touching each other.

"Let's do it. Right here," Gino whispered.

My prior intimacies had my hormones on high alert, and I was curious. But this experience became uncomfortable very quickly.

"I've never had sex yet. Don't really know what to do," I told him as he touched and fumbled around.

It was like a switch flipped.

"I'll do you from behind," he growled.

Spinning me around, he pushed me forward. With my pants already undone, he swiftly pulled them over my butt. As he tried to enter, panic hit, and the fog of the alcohol began lifting through sheer fear.

"Stop! You're hurting me! Stop," I screamed, but he wouldn't let me go. With my arms pinned and my face smashed into the tree, he finished.

When he finally let loose, I pulled up my pants and ran without looking back as he laughed and teased.

"Ah, don't be mad. I'll do better next time."

Mortified with myself, I stumbled into the barracks, trying to be as quiet as possible, and went straight to the bathroom to throw up. Bleeding and sore, I crawled into my rack and cried myself to sleep.

*

The next day was rough, but I muddled through. Not knowing who to turn to or how, I didn't say a word to anyone about what happened.

Sitting on a curb outside the barracks after school, a pair of boots stopped beside me, and I looked up into the face of another schoolmate. He sat down next to me.

"Are you okay?"

"Yeah, why?" It was kind of a snap, like go away.

"I'm Keith."

Not feeling the introduction and invasion of space, I just looked at him.

"I'm Gino's best friend."

Wanting to get up and run, I put my head in my hands instead, hoping that maybe if I couldn't see anything this would all go away. Keith touched me gently on the shoulder.

"Gino told me about what happened last night."

"What did he say?" I managed to ask with big tears welling up.

"He came flying into the barracks, boasting about popping the cherry of a virgin," he said softly. "Said you were drunk. Even told us you asked him to stop, that he was hurting you."

Humiliation set in. Shame and tears flowed.

"Who's us?" I managed to choke out.

"There were a bunch of us in the room playing D&D."

Keith just let me sob.

"I'm married," he finally broke in. "When he told us about what he did, I was pissed. I thought about my wife and daughter. I'd kill anyone who treated either of them like that. Please take care of yourself. Make better choices."

I carried the shame for decades. Even though relationships came, I struggled with closeness and feeling good about myself, especially sexually. Once I was in a relationship and sex became more intimate, I shut down, not knowing how to go deeper without feeling ashamed and dirty. I was going through the motions to make my partner happy, but I found no sexual release myself.

* * *

The story of life—making choices, good and bad.

Afraid to turn to God, ashamed and embarrassed, I didn't get the true meaning of all-knowing and omnipresent. I just figured that if I didn't say it or talk about it, He wouldn't know.

> *Where can I go from your Spirit? Where can I flee from your presence? If I go up to the heavens, you are there; if I make my bed in the depths, you are there. If I rise on the wings of the dawn, if I settle on the far side of the sea, even there your hand will guide me, your right hand will hold me fast. If I say, "Surely the darkness will hide me and the light become night around me," even the darkness will not be dark to you; the night will shine like the day, for darkness is as light to you.*[2]

David wrote those words in a song, a psalm, to the Lord knowing God is always with us, and there is no hiding place. He is there with us anyplace we can find, waiting with the patience only

He has. David penned six very loaded verses telling of the Spirit and presence of God. They are both in the heavens and the depths. In other versions, the word *depths* is translated "Sheol," meaning death or the grave. Jesus conquered death. David didn't know that at the time, but we have the honor.

David knew he couldn't outrun the rising of the sun because God is light. If he crossed the sea, God would guide him. Even in the dark, God would be his light.

So why do we think we can hide?

* * *

Throwing my shoulders back, I did what I knew how to do and pushed forward. I put my head down and studied.

"Anything I can help you with?"

Looking up in annoyance, I checked myself because the Marine smiling from the other side of the break room stopped me breathing. Doing a double take, I had to make sure I wasn't dreaming because he resembled a young Richard Gere leaning against the vending machine with a Cactus Cooler in his hand.

"Hi." He gave me a finger wave with the hand holding the soda. "I'm Paul."

"I'm Traci." Stuck on something, I went for it. "The theory isn't registering for me on this project."

"Bet I can have you on track by the time we go back in," he challenged, walking over and sitting next to me. He had on English Leather cologne, Dad's favorite.

By the time our break was over, Paul was able to give me a much better understanding of the schematic that had been kicking my butt.

*

"Hey! You lost the bet." He caught up to me after class. He had a cocky side smile.

"We didn't shake on anything," I teased.

"Ah, that's wrong. See, I should get something in return for my time, my knowledge."

Narrowing my eyes at him and trying not to laugh, he added, "Not to mention my good looks." Then we both started cracking up.

"What would you have asked for—if we had bet?"

He put his chin on his knuckles, mimicking thinking.

"I'm not sure what it would have been. But now, I'd just like to walk you to the barracks." Then he tipped his head as if to say *please grant my humble request*. It was sweet.

On the way, Paul shared about growing up in Delaware and that he has a sister. They were raised by his mom and stepdad, who were both functioning alcoholics. He didn't have much contact with his biological dad and joined the service as a way to turn things around after getting in trouble at home.

"I've really enjoyed talking with you. Don't want to stop. Do you have stuff to do right now?" he asked as we approached the barracks.

"Just study. What'd you have in mind?"

"Let's study together." He pointed at a picnic table area.

We talked about everything but homework.

* * *

After a couple weeks, I told Paul about Gino.

"I'm really sorry that happened to you." He seemed genuinely upset by it. "I didn't know you . . . " He trailed off, started pacing, and then stopped in front of me. His voice softened. "I was there that night."

He paused to let it sink in, but I wasn't sure if he was referring to the bowling alley or the barracks. Then he went on, almost as if in thought, recalling the night.

"I was in another room with a bunch of guys playing D&D. It was late. A bunch of other dudes came bursting in saying . . . I had no idea you were who . . . " He sat down beside me, pulling me close.

"I didn't know Gino, but whatever he said didn't go over well. Some of the guys wanted to kick his ass," he said sweetly into my hair. "You have to shake that off," he encouraged.

* * *

We connected with each other, enjoyed being together, and began dating. When I thought I trusted him enough, Paul made my second sexual experience much more pleasant. Then way too soon in our relationship, we got engaged. Paul proposed at "our picnic table." At the time, we thought we had it all figured out.

We took vacation together to meet each other's families. Alice and Shupe were nice, although never sober. They loved beer and drank it like some people drink coffee—first thing in the morning and all through the day. Paul's family was incredibly happy for us. Alice jumped in and asked to have the wedding at their house.

"That would be nice," I said. What did I know? As soon as the words came out of my mouth, she dove in and started making arrangements. Her care was foreign and made me uncomfortable, awkward.

We drove to Jamestown. It was a tense visit. I was very uncomfortable bringing something good into a place I never thought of as home. As we pulled into the lower driveway, I looked up at my former bedroom window. An intense sadness hit, and suddenly I had no idea what I was doing and wanted to run.

Dad and Lil liked Paul but voiced their skepticism about our getting married without feeling things out longer. It didn't faze us, but Paul felt the weight in the house, too.

Things were different than the last visit. There was strain between Dad and Lil, and we barely saw Todd. Alice called while we were there. She had found some great deals on vehicles, and that gave us an excuse to leave early. We let Lil and Dad know we didn't want to miss out on a potentially good find and jammed out as fast as we could.

Back at school, we put our noses to the grindstone studying because finals were closing in and we'd be graduating soon. Neither of us had any idea where our assignments would take us, except I knew I'd be somewhere on the West Coast.

* * *

Headed for Camp Pendleton, I left Tennessee before Paul. He was off to Tustin. We were close, about 50 miles apart, but it was still a problem with no driver's license or car.

After reporting in and being assigned a barrack, I began training for my regular job.

Paul and I finally got to meet up for Thanksgiving.

9

A year had gone by since I spent my most miserable Thanksgiving alone. Rolling along confused, I tried to be happy with where I was in life, but I had a lot of questions and no idea how or who to ask. I wanted guidance, but I didn't trust anyone because it would mean letting them in, even just a little, and that scared me.

When I tried to check in with Dad one day, Lil answered, so we chatted. After catching up, she asked, "Did you hear about Terry?"

"No, I haven't heard anything from him in a while. What's up?"

"When did you last talk to him?"

"After boot camp."

"Terry died."

It was blunt and to the point. I thought my knees were going to buckle because I had recently discovered that I'd lost his necklace.

"What happened?" I finally asked after a long pause.

"It's not clear yet. It's still being investigated. The news said he was killed by his brother during a fight."

"Does Jimmy know?"

"He's the one who told me. Then I caught it on TV."

We said goodbye, and I hung up without talking to Dad. I went for a walk to clear my head. My own insecurities and immaturity had pushed Terry away without even knowing what his intentions really were. He had always treated me with kindness and respect. The news hit me hard, and I felt awful for how I had treated him. My mood grew dark.

Then I humiliated myself by failing the first physical fitness test, or PFT as we called it. I didn't complete the run on time. It was my own fault. I hadn't been training, and I was down in the dumps and struggling. I was assigned to a special class. We ran the hills behind the barracks every day, which was rough.

Wanting to get back in proper form and pull myself together, I got into weight lifting with a friend. He worked with me to get in shape, and I passed the next PFT, although not with a gold star.

Paul and I saw each other on weekends—not always every weekend, but we did the best we could. Eventually, he bought a car, a '76 Trans Am. It was in good shape on the outside, but we soon learned it wasn't mechanically sound. Although the Trans Am didn't last long, I was finally able to get my driver's license before it went kaput.

*

Excited to be engaged, I wasn't prepared for how quickly things were moving along. Not knowing how to communicate, I held it all in.

Alice was a wonderful woman and so happy about her son getting married, but in her excitement, she never took me or even Paul into consideration. She just took over planning the entire wedding, including the date. She'd call us about our choices for this or that, and we'd just pick something or leave it up to her because we were busy trying to integrate into the service.

A few months before the wedding, I was sent to Cherry Point, North Carolina, for more schooling on a different type of equipment. At Alice's request, I grudgingly took a long weekend to visit before I left.

After a detailed rundown of wedding eve and day, the big item to check off her list was the dress. We went shopping, but I questioned myself the entire time about what I was doing, unsure where I was going in life and what I wanted.

*

The summer of '86 came around way too fast. Uncomfortable with the attention and people being excited, I was just going through the motions. "Cold feet" may be the most appropriate phrase. I wanted to run as far away from the scene as fast as possible. As more and more family and friends came into town, my apprehension grew. Alice had been in contact with Lil, and "family" I didn't even know had been invited.

The night before the ceremony, Alice and Shupe arranged for a huge crab shindig at a local restaurant. I was starting to relax and actually enjoy myself when the drama hit.

One of Paul's ex-girlfriends, Trish, had been in and around the scene the entire time. It didn't bother me until the night of the dinner when Dorothy came over.

"So, I've been told Trish is still interested in Paul. She's been trying to throw a wrench in your plans."

"Where'd you hear that?" My calm remained, but a flutter in my gut went off.

"From her. She said when Paul tells you he's taking off with his buddies, he's really going to see her."

Not trusting Dorothy, I didn't believe it and kept what she told me to myself—for the time being.

Later that evening when everyone returned to the house, I spoke with Mark and relayed what Dorothy told me.

"Eh, I don't know about all that. She might've just been trying to start something. After you left, I had it out with her. She was pretty pissed off with you. Don't know if she still is, but I'd take that with a grain of salt."

Dorothy never said a word to me.

*

The day of the wedding arrived. While we were waiting to head outside, I turned to the one constant in my life.

"Dad, I'm not ready to do this."

"Oh, you're fine, just nervous," he joked back while fixing the sleeve of his jacket.

"No, Dad." I grabbed his arm so he'd look at me eye-to-eye. "I really don't want to get married. I'm not ready for all this."

His facial expression fell, and he got flush. He was mad.

"Don't you think you should've spoken up sooner? Look outside!" He grabbed my arm and pulled me to the screen door, pointing. "Do you see everything Alice has done?"

"I know, but it's not what I wanted. I don't know what I want, but I don't want to get married right now."

He reached over, and thinking he was going to hit me, I flinched. Pushing my shoulders back, he turned me around and pointed again.

"You're in it. All those people are out there for you."

Then he shoved me out the door.

*

I tried to relax during the hubbub after the ceremony, but that went out the window when Trish came walking up.

"Can we talk?" she asked. "I need to tell you something."

"Go ahead."

She gave me a snotty "tsk" and then shifted her hips and popped her neck.

"After the crab dinner last night, after you went to bed and before Paul left for Matt's, he hooked up with Dorothy."

"What do you mean hooked up?"

"Dorothy told me they had sex in the pool."

"Dorothy told you?"

"Yeah."

Walking away from her without another word, I got a flutter back in my gut. It was just too strange. Something had to be going on between Trish and Dorothy. With no idea if it was true, I kept it to myself.

*

Eventually, Paul and I made the escape to spend our wedding night together.

When we got to the hotel, I coyly did some "investigating."

"Dorothy said she thinks Trish still has the hots for you." It was a playful tease while Paul removed his jacket.

"Maybe, but that was over a long time ago," he returned, walking over to me while peeling off his shirt.

"What do you think of Dorothy?"

He grabbed me by the forearms, pulling me to him, and kissed my neck softly, starting at the cleft in my collar bone.

"She's all right, but kind of skanky," he said in my ear. "Now . . ." He gently pushed me back a little by the shoulders so we were looking into each other's eyes. "Will you stop talking?"

His kiss and attention were what any woman would dream of, especially on her wedding night. What was I to think?

* * *

We'd been hoping to find a good deal on a truck, and then we found one. Driving back to California, we got to do some sightseeing and talk about the future, our dreams, and our plans. It was the first time in a while that I felt like everything was going to be all right, that we could do this—that I could. Excited to start life together, we powered through the end of the drive so we could have time to unwind. Still at separate bases, we had that to contend with until we submitted the paperwork to be able to live off base.

Once approval came through, apartment hunting began close to Tustin pending my petition to be reassigned either there or to El Toro.

Moving day was a Saturday. We were ecstatic. Starting with my stuff and then working our way to the new apartment, we made a game of it, having fun, joking, and laughing. By mid-afternoon, we were in and unpacking. The bedroom got set up first—well, just the bed. Then we broke it in.

* * *

Paul was in the living room unpacking a box, so I dove into the bedroom stuff. We had half-heartedly thrown the bed together, so I was fixing it and almost missed the folded piece of paper camouflaged against the sheets. Thinking it was something Paul had left for me, I picked it up and then caught a scent of fragrance. My stomach dropped.

Before opening it, I knew I didn't want to. Her handwriting was beautiful, and so were the first words. "I love you, Paul. Always have." It was signed "Love, Trish." I paced the room about 20 times before walking out into the living room.

"What's this?" I yelled, the note raised in my hand.

Paul jumped and turned, and then his face fell.

"It's nothing. She gave it to me before we left."

"When exactly did that happen? I didn't see her come around before we took off."

"Out with Matt one day." He tried to brush me off and go back to unpacking the box.

"Liar! Dorothy told me what you were really up to when you said you were out with Matt. It says it right here." Crumpling the note, I screamed, "You still have feelings for her. Why were you sneaking off to see her? What else went on?"

"What?"

"Why'd you keep it?" I dug in.

He glared at me.

"You'd better check yourself. You put *this* under your pillow in the bed we just made love in." I held my fist with the wadded-up note in front of his face, and we stared at each other for a minute. "Were you with Dorothy after the crab dinner?"

Paul stepped forward, slammed me backward into the wall, and then quickly stepped back. All the joy and happiness from just a short half an hour before were now unrecognizable, and I just stood there, not knowing what to say or do.

"I'm so sorry. I didn't mean to shove you," he immediately apologized.

It made no sense, and instantly I shut down, blamed myself, and bore the shame and guilt. He'd been with both women, but I felt like I'd done something wrong.

Paul tried harder than I did to make it work after that. My mistrust was too deep. Not feeling safe, I withdrew into myself and went silent. We just coexisted.

To have my own space, I volunteered for the night shift at Pendleton. It lasted until the transfer to El Toro, a transfer I wished I had never requested.

* * *

Avionics was run much differently at El Toro. The officers and heads in charge were openly and very blatantly sexist. The base had been dubbed "The Boys Club."

Initiation to my new division came by way of the officer in charge tagging me to become his secretary. Fighting the assignment, I was sent to mess duty and told that everyone had to serve in the mess hall. But there were rumors it was punishment for refusing to be reassigned.

Once back at avionics, I was pressured again. But then I was not given a choice.

Digging my heels in, I learned and actually liked the job. I let the BAM (broad ass Marine) comments and other sexual jokes and innuendos concerning the female anatomy roll off my shoulders.

* * *

And more time together wasn't helping my marriage to Paul. We grew unhappier and argued over money, his spending, and his use of credit cards. During the drive back from the East Coast, we talked about saving for another vehicle, but we had become so disconnected that the idea went out the window.

A bond purchased with most of my savings before leaving for the service paid out. I had put the money away for a motorcycle, so that's exactly what I bought, without even knowing how to ride. Paul rode it home.

Once I was comfortable driving the motorcycle, it was a source of freedom for me, my escape from a crap marriage. It renewed my love of being outdoors. In the silence of a ride with just the hum of the tires, I felt closer to God again, searching. But I was too scared to reach out—afraid and ashamed.

*

One evening after one of my rides, Paul wanted to talk. He looked serious, so I sat down across from him at the table.

"I'm being deployed."

We knew it could happen. It's something we had discussed before everything fell apart. Now a reality, it didn't seem so bad to hear. It was almost a relief.

"When?"

"January."

"Where to?"

"Japan. On a ship for six months." He looked worried.

"Are you scared?"

"I'll only have five months left when I get back."

"Yeah." I wasn't sure where he was going with it.

"I'm going back home after discharge."

"That's fine. I'm not going with you. We'll figure it out when the time comes."

So that was it. The end was in sight.

*

With time to myself, I got back to working out. A PFT was coming up. One of my coworkers, Steve, was into the gym scene and bodybuilding. We connected on that level and got to know one another a little. One day, he asked me out for a beer.

"What's your story?" he asked as we sat down.

"What do you mean, service-wise?"

"No," he smiled and laughed. "You wear a ring but have never mentioned a husband."

"It's not worth mentioning." It should have been left at that, but then I blurted out, "Same with you. You talk about your daughter, never your wife."

"It's complicated. I've been hanging in there, but . . . " his voice trailed off. Not knowing each other's exact pain, we felt it and found comfort in one other as we shared our marital hurts. Then we switched gears and talked about hobbies, bikes, staying fit, and military life.

"I really don't want this to end." Steve took my hand in his and just held it. It seemed like such a caring gesture. "I've enjoyed talking with you. It's been a while since I've felt this relaxed."

His hands were huge and engulfed mine. Raising my eyes to his, I wondered if he had a violent side. The thought jolted me.

"We'd better roll," I said, slipping my hand out of his. I grabbed my helmet and stood up.

Steve walked me to my bike. While I was swinging my leg over, he caught my arm and stopped me.

"Wait," he held on, letting me regain my balance. Then he turned me to face him.

"I just . . . " he started to say and then gently pulled me close, eased his other hand to the nape of my neck, and steered me in for a kiss. It was smooth, and my heart jumped.

As we pulled away from each other, Steve tugged on a strand of my hair.

"Can we do this again?"

Stepping back and tapping him in the abs playfully with my helmet, it was hard not to smile.

"Definitely. See you tomorrow."

"Definitely," he mimicked. "Be careful," he said loudly as my bike came to life.

Riding off excited, feeling warm and fuzzy inside, I pulled into the carport not feeling good about myself. The mind games began. I knew what an affair felt like from a kid's perspective, and now as an adult, I was seeing it from the other side of a hurtful, failed relationship—how it happens, the emotions and feelings involved. Then justification started. My marriage was long over, Paul had cheated, we weren't intimate anymore, blah, blah.

*

Steve and I began flirting at work, getting a thrill out of gently touching hands or nudging one another throughout the day, trying to stay on the down-low.

"Listen," Steve said one day as I set a piece of equipment down beside him. "Dawn's out of town." It was the first time he'd said his wife's name. "Would you like to come over tonight?" The look in his eyes was sultry.

"Yes."

Justification won, and I believed it would feel good to relax and enjoy someone.

"I'll give you a call when I'm home from the gym, probably around 8:00. Good?"

"Good."

*

I knocked on his door, and his hulk-like frame stood in front of me. With clothes on, he was impressive. But seeing him shirtless. . . . He was freshly pumped from his evening workout, muscles taut, ripe with fresh blood flow and adrenaline. Abs on point, he knew how to get my attention standing there in just a pair of sweatpants.

"Come in," he said.

His apartment was warm and nicely decorated—not his touch, probably hers, I thought.

"Want something to drink?"

"Just water, please."

Pictures caught my attention, so I walked into the living room to check out a display on a table. As the photos came into view, I stopped. Not wanting to see them as a family, I turned around and went back to the kitchen entryway just as Steve came out.

"How was the ride?" he asked.

He carried our glasses, nodding for me to follow, and then pulled me down beside him on the couch. There was a basketball game on, but he turned the sound down.

"Not a lot of traffic, pretty smooth."

He situated himself so he was turned toward me, his arm on the head of the couch above me.

"You're pretty smooth," he commented.

Dropping his arm down around me, he pulled me close. He smelled clean, intoxicating, his breath fresh.

"How am I smooth?" I giggled and teased.

"Because you smell so good right now, I can't even think." His breath was warm as he leaned in for a kiss. His hands strong and guiding, we melted into each other.

Steve quickly pulled away, stood up while pulling me to my feet, scooped me in his arms, carried me into the bedroom, and then gently laid me on the bed and turned to shut the door. Quickly removing my shoes, he took me by the hands, pulled me back up to my feet, and then swiftly removed my shirt. He laid me back down and then crawled up over the top of me, gently kissing my belly and making me giggle at the tickle of his scruff.

"Shhh," he whispered quietly. The room went silent. "The baby's in the other room."

He felt me go stiff, so we sat up.

"Your daughter's here?" I whispered back loudly.

"She's asleep. We just have to keep it down."

He pressed into me, playfully pinning me down, and I succumbed to the temptation.

*

"I'd better get going."

"Not yet." He propped himself up on an elbow so we could make eye contact.

"It's a little weird that you didn't tell me that Ashley was here."

Staring at the ceiling, he turned my face toward him. "She doesn't know anything. We'll make sure to get up before she does. The alarm's set for 4:00. Don't go yet." He playfully tickled me. "I'm not done. Are you?"

*

He fell asleep, but I couldn't. As 3:00 a.m. clicked on the display, I silently dressed and snuck out of the apartment, knowing I wouldn't be back. Steve didn't know my upbringing, and I didn't know his. Explaining what it feels like when a little girl finds out her dad isn't everything he's supposed to be wasn't something I felt up to.

The ringing of the phone woke me that Saturday morning.

"Why didn't you wake me?" He sounded groggy.

"Couldn't sleep, and you were zonked, so I showed myself out."

"What are your plans today?"

"Don't have any really."

"Can I see you?"

"I thought she was coming home today."

"She is. I pick her up at 11:00. We should be home by noon. Meet me at the coffee shop down the hill at 1:00."

*

Curious, I left early, parked across from his apartment a little before noon, and waited. Then I watched as Steve, his wife, and daughter pulled up and began unloading luggage from the car. It was a happy family scene as Ashley ran around her mom, excited that she was home.

As I left to head down the hill, I rode right past them. Dawn and Ashley had no clue who I was unless they caught the look of recognition and shock on Steve's face.

"What was that?" He was a little miffed when he arrived at the coffee shop.

"What? They don't know? I wanted to see how you guys are together. Seems like a happy family to me." It was cocky.

"I can assure you it's all show for the baby's sake."

"Well, I can assure you that for the baby's sake, I won't be coming around anymore." It was snotty, but it really bothered me that he referred to his daughter as the baby when she was three going on four.

"Don't say that."

"I'm not comfortable coming to your place."

"Then I'll come to yours."

*

Our interest in each other was pretty much physical. There wasn't any desire to go out and do stuff together. We weren't concerned about future things; we were just living in the moment, having fun, I thought. We saw each other at work and whenever he could come over.

About a month into it, Steve's scary side surfaced by way of a temper that could flare instantly. He never mistreated me, but there were times he'd show up when something was off with him.

"What's up with you?" I asked him one night when he was all hyped up.

"Nothing. Just came from the gym."

"Exercise doesn't do that to me. You're like pumped up and ready to punch someone. It's making me nervous."

"I'm sorry. I don't mean to come off like that." With his hype deflated, he paused in thought and then confessed. "I use steroids. They can get me going."

Knowing nothing about steroids, I knew the mood swings he went through when he used them, and it turned me off. We remained friends but stopped seeing each other.

* * *

After passing the next PFT, I continued hitting the gym on my own and then found out what can happen when you don't have a spotter. While using the elevated leg press machine and pushing the weight up, my legs went suddenly weak. Trying to bring the weight back down, my knee caps popped and slid to the outside. With my legs locked and still holding the weight, I had to smack the caps back into place, slamming the weight down.

My right knee swelled within minutes, the left just slightly. Carefully scooting out of the seat onto the floor, I butt-crawled over to the Jacuzzi and hung my legs in the water. About 20 minutes later, my legs felt like jelly, but I was able to walk. Once home, I rested and iced. The next morning, my left knee seemed back to normal, but the right one was still swollen. Taking it easy for a while, I kept icing, and eventually, everything went back to normal.

A few weeks later, while participating in a Memorial Day fun run with my division, I went down about three-quarters of the way through. My right knee had dislocated again. I went to the hospital, and the doctor put me on bed rest and referred me to orthopedics. A few days later, I had a full leg cast.

Paul was due home about a week before the cast was to come off. We hadn't talked much, only during the first month. Neighbors drove me in our truck to pick him up and then left so we could have some alone time. Although not excited, I was looking forward to seeing him because he was familiar.

Coming down the tarmac with his uniform hanging, he looked emaciated and smiled weakly as he approached. He looked like death—gaunt and yellow.

He caught sight of the cast, and his eyes widened. We must have been a sight. He had no idea of my ventures, and I had no idea he had contracted a form of hepatitis.

Our relationship wasn't good, but we remained cordial. Out of loneliness and reaching for something, we attempted to be intimate one evening, but it was sex with no feeling behind it.

When it was time for my cast to come off, we were both in shock at the state of my leg—no muscle tone, shrunken, pasty white, and hairy. Standing up to walk, I knew it didn't feel right, and orthoscopic surgery was scheduled.

In the meantime, Paul's discharge went through. He found a job, hung on until I recovered from surgery, and then headed home. Our goodbye was easy. We told each other we'd figure out the rest later.

* * *

I added the shame and guilt of being a failure in marriage to the pit where I had shoved my other hurts and pains. Trusting Paul after I had been raped was huge, but after his cheating and lies, further and further down the rabbit hole I went, looking for love in all the wrong places.

Those who live according to the flesh have their minds set on what the flesh desires; but those who live in accordance with the Spirit have their minds set on what the Spirit desires. The mind governed by the flesh is death, but the mind governed by the Spirit is life and peace. The mind governed by the flesh is hostile to God; it does not submit to God's law, nor can it do so. Those who are in the realm of the flesh cannot please God.[1]

Had I turned to God . . .

Trust in the LORD with all your heart, and do not lean on your own understanding. In all your ways acknowledge him, and he will make straight your paths.[2]

My paths were far from straight.

10

Surgery on my knee didn't help much, and the doctors recommended a replacement. After hearing what was involved, I declined. That ended my service career because I could no longer perform the necessary physical requirements. As my squadron prepared to leave for Desert Shield, I was sent to the Medical Review Board pending discharge.

At one of my doctors' appointments, I met Leslie and Bala, a couple who lived about three miles from me. Bala was in the service, and Leslie was his civilian wife. We hit it off, and they invited me for dinner.

They had two beautiful little girls and were a fun family. Leslie and I became friends. Since I wasn't working, I enjoyed spending time with her and their girls. As I got to know them, though, all wasn't well. Maybe it should have been a clue for my next wrong choice.

How their marriage imploded is a mystery, but as I got to know Leslie, I found out she was a partier. People were constantly in and out of their house.

"Where's Bala been?" I asked one day after realizing he hadn't been around in a while.

"Dunno. He got pissed off one night, took off, and went AWOL. He's all freaked out about being deployed. It's crazy." Leslie was baking chocolate chip cookies and brought one my way on a spatula.

"Are you and the girls doing okay?"

"We're fine. Better off." She paused, put her hands flat on the counter, and blew out a breath. "I don't really know what's going to happen."

"Hang in there. It will all work out. Bala will show up, and . . ." I didn't know what else to say. "It will all just work out."

"A night out is what I need." She pushed back from the counter and started dancing. "A few of us are headed out tomorrow night. You in?"

*

It was 1989. Dresses were tight, heels were high, and so was hair. It took about a quarter can of hairspray to get the look right. We were done up for a girl's night out, me in flats because my knee said no to heels.

After we found a table and ordered drinks, Leslie leaned over.

"Hey, Carter's here." She pointed across the way.

Carter was a friend of hers who showed up every now and then. I had taken notice but kept it to myself, wanting time before another relationship. That didn't last long.

"He asked about you," Leslie said as she coyly took a sip of her drink.

"Asked?" I gave her the rolling hand signal for more information please.

"Your status. I told him you're going through a divorce."

It made me cringe. Paul and I had always danced around the word. We chose the phrase "take care of things" instead. Leslie didn't know a lot about my situation—just a few specifics, no details.

"Are you going to get a divorce?" I asked her out of the blue.

She slowly nodded yes and then said, "Probably."

"How's that make you feel?"

"Whoa! Are you going to share, 'cuz you're a pretty guarded Marine." She side-eyed me, raised her drink, and said, "That's what this is for. How does it make you feel?"

It wasn't going to come out of my mouth. Searching for a neutral word, I took a cue from her and said, "Numb." But it wasn't her kind of numb. It was the cave within where I hid, where I could sit in darkness and beat myself up with shame, guilt, and failure. I was living that way on the inside and trying to keep going on the outside, choosing to be alone with what was within.

Leslie narrowed her eyes at me and leaned back as if she were looking me over, studying me, being funny.

"That was a share?"

We clinked drinks and laughed.

"But back to Carter. He asked because he's interested."

Carter and I had chatted a few times here and there. He was extremely attractive, in shape, blonde, and blue-eyed, and he had a fabulous smile. He made me sweat with nervousness.

Leslie nudged me as he approached the table a few minutes later and greeted us with a smile.

"Ladies, nice seeing you."

He took Leslie's hand, led her out of her seat, and then said, "Turn."

Leslie giggled and modeled for him.

"Fabulous!" he exclaimed and ushered her back to her seat.

He put out his hand for me to take. Looking at him cautiously, he tipped his hand a little closer, urging me to take it. As I did, he tugged lightly for me to stand.

He led me out a couple of steps and then let go of my hand.

"You have the most amazing green eyes." He leaned in a little as he slowly began circling, checking me out. As he came back in front of me, he sucked in his breath and held it, being dramatic, and slowly said, "Breathtaking" as he blew a kiss into the air. He was charming.

Carter sat me back down and asked, "May I?"

He sat beside me, and as the night wore on, he shared that he lived with his grandmother and was helping care for her while going to school and working part time. He seemed like an on-the-ball go-getter.

"How did you and Leslie meet?" I asked as Leslie came back to the table. She heard me and laughed.

"We met at school." Carter laughed, too.

"I tried going back to school but failed miserably," Leslie admitted. "Too hard with the kids and everything." Her glass went up in the air again. Her divorce toast became the theme of the night.

Carter and I had an amazing time talking, laughing, and dancing. He was not only handsome but smart and had a great sense of humor—in the beginning anyway.

Our attraction seemed mutual. We flirted, and then at one point, he came up behind me and softly ran his finger up one of my legs. An exciting shiver went all the way to the top of my head. Turning to him, we kissed.

It was right—until it all eventually went wrong.

*

During one of our first solo conversations, I asked Carter about his family, and he crinkled his nose.

"We're not that tight."

"Why not?"

"We're going in deep right off the bat, huh?" he smiled. "I've always clashed with my parents, felt second-rate to my brother."

"Is it just you and your brother?"

"Yeah."

"Younger or older?"

"Younger. He's always been the favorite."

"Does it affect your relationship with him?"

"Sometimes. We've sparred, but I love Chris. He's my bro."

"Are your parents still together?"

"Yeah. They're in Orange. I visit every now and then. You'll meet them."

And I did, about a month later. We were driving around on a Saturday.

"Wanna meet my parents?"

"Now?" I was caught off guard.

"Now," he grinned at my unease.

"But we should call ahead first, let them know we're coming."

"I already did." His full-blown smile set me at ease.

Joyce and Norm seemed like fabulous people. Their greeting was warm and kind. Chris was completely different from Carter as far as looks go. Carter was lean and muscular; Chris was taller, thick, and muscular. The entire family treated me wonderfully. It was a completely different vibe than when I'd met Paul's family. There was no overbearing excitement over an engagement. We were just relaxed and comfortable.

As Joyce showed me around their home, it wasn't hard to notice that there were no pictures of Carter anywhere. There were all kinds of family pictures and ones of Chris, but none of Carter.

I asked Carter about it afterward.

"It's like I told you. I've always had an on-off relationship with my parents. Chris is the golden boy."

Running my hand along the side of his face, I hoped to wipe the look of hurt away.

"I'm glad I found you." He grabbed my hand and kissed it.

We connected in that moment. At least I did, thinking he was a child of the back seat like me. I thought my most prayed for wish had come true and I'd found someone who loved me and would treat me right. Relaxed, I felt safe to open up to him, share my pain, and tell him about my upbringing—all of it, my mom's illness, my dad's violence, things I hadn't shared with Paul. I told Carter about Paul, how our relationship died.

He pulled off to the side of the road and softly kissed me.

"We have each other now," he whispered, and we just sat there for a few minutes.

"Have you thought about moving in together?" He broke the silence.

"What about your grandmother?"

"She's recovered from surgery and on her feet. I'll talk to her about it."

"I didn't know she had surgery."

"It's why I've been helping her out." He pulled a stray strand of hair away from my cheek. "So, what do you say?"

"Yes." Thinking I'd found the man of my dreams, I added, "But let's find our own place."

Not wanting to stay in the apartment I had shared with Paul, we moved.

*

Soon after we moved, I started bleeding abnormally. The base doctor couldn't find a reason and did a pregnancy test, but it was negative.

Another week went by, and still they couldn't find anything wrong. But this time they tested for pregnancy by blood, not urine. It was positive. But something was wrong.

The doctor was alarmed that it might be an ectopic pregnancy. With no idea what that meant, I quickly learned the fertilized egg was stuck in a fallopian tube. It wasn't good, especially with all the time that had gone by. The base's medical community wasn't equipped to handle such an emergency, so I was sent directly to an off-site hospital.

I never wanted to have children because of what Mom had gone through. But when the word *pregnant* hit my ears, my thinking stumbled. Completely thrown for a loop and scared out of my mind, I wanted to turn to God, but the curse reared its ugly head, and I felt damned.

So I turned to Carter. He too was in shock.

"I'm on my way. Be there in half an hour." He sounded concerned.

"I'm okay. This should be fast. Just wait, I'll fill you in when I get home."

"You sure?"

"Yeah. They're waiting for me, so I'll know something soon."

A tubal pregnancy was confirmed. Surgery was scheduled for the next morning. Life was spinning. Arriving at our apartment, I laid it on Carter.

"There's no way to save it?" he asked.

"There's nothing they can do."

We slept very little. Carter took me to the hospital early the next morning. He was very solemn. At the time, I thought it was sweet.

"You're lucky. The operation went fine," the surgeon told me in recovery. "Fallopian tubes are only about the width of a strand of hair. Yours was stretched to its limit, but I was able to leave it intact."

Already on no duty, I was put on bed rest for six weeks. Carter and Chris helped see me through the first couple of weeks, which were the most painful.

* * *

I never told anyone about my loss. It was more shame to carry, something else to hide.

While I was still married to Paul, I was living with Carter and pregnant by him. The Word gives a pretty good example of what the outcome of my choices could be.

I'll paraphrase one story.

When a married King David took the night off from battle and hooked up with Bathsheba, she became pregnant. Then David arranged to have her husband killed on the battlefield to try to cover up their indiscretion.

Then he married Bathsheba and attempted to continue on like nothing had happened, but it was driving him nuts. In ancient times, people didn't have the gift of the Holy Spirit. God spoke through chosen people—prophets. The prophet Nathan warned David of his sins and coming judgment.

David repented, saving his own life, but God's judgment fell on the baby Bathsheba gave birth to, and the baby became ill. David fasted and prayed, but the baby died.[1]

God loves and knows everyone intimately. He knows everything about us—how we're conceived, our circumstances, what we're going to go through, how long we'll live, all of it.

> *For you formed my inward parts; you knitted me together in my mother's womb. I praise you, for I am fearfully and wonderfully made. Wonderful are your works; my soul knows it very well. My frame was not hidden from you, when I was being made in secret, intricately woven in the depths of the earth. Your eyes saw my unformed substance; in your book were written, every one of them, the days that were formed for me, when as yet there was none of them.*[2]

King David, in his conviction and repentance, knew he'd see his child again.

> *Then his servants said to him, "What is this thing that you have done? You fasted and wept for the child while he was alive; but when the child died, you arose and ate food." He said, "While the child was still alive, I fasted and wept, for I said, 'Who knows whether the LORD will be gracious to me, that the child may live?' But now he is dead. Why should I fast? Can I bring him back again? I shall go to him, but he will not return to me."*[3]

David knew he had been forgiven because Nathan told him the Lord forgave him. He knew he would see his son again.

When I cry at the memory of it all now, they aren't tears of pain and shame. They're tears of joy at the overwhelming grace and forgiveness given to me, to all of us, through the blood of Jesus. I too will meet the child I lost. The value of that kind of knowledge turns to wisdom and keeps you on the narrow path.

But there was still some of the broader path to go.

* * *

While I was home recuperating from surgery, Carter's demeanor changed. He lost his job, became quick-tempered and moody, and went through bouts of depression. The flutter in my gut kicked in.

"Can I borrow some money for cigarettes?" Carter asked one day while we were standing in our bathroom.

"We have to make sure we have rent first," I reminded him.

The words were barely out of my mouth when the shove came. He hit me in my chest flat handed with both hands, with so much force that it threw me back against the wall.

I wasn't aware of what happened right away, and I couldn't figure out where I was. As my head cleared, the realization that I was lying on the floor of the closet sank in. The door wouldn't open; there was something blocking it.

Lying there shaking and petrified, I felt destined to live Mom's life.

"Why, God? Why is it like this for me? Why aren't You with me?" I finally cried out and sobbed.

*

My misery was interrupted by sound. Someone had come in through the back door from the carport. Something clunked, and the closet door opened. There stood Carter in all his evil glory, so ugly for being such a beautiful man.

He had calmed down some, but his eyes were still glassy and full of rage. He just stood there looking at me and then barked, "Go ahead and try to leave."

Sitting there a mess, I didn't say a word. After a couple of minutes, he turned on his heel and said, "Let's go."

As we entered the dining room, he nudged his chin toward the back door.

"Try to leave," he said teasingly.

My bike was the first thought. As calmly as possible, I walked to the back door and looked out into the carport. It was gone.

"What'd you do with it?"

"It's gone," he said, waving his arms like a magician.

"Will you please bring it back?"

"Are you going to try to leave?" He started to soften.

Exhausted, I couldn't argue, and my head was killing me. Dizziness hit like I was going to faint.

"I'm not going to leave. I need to lie down. Please go get it," I pleaded. Then I turned and went into the bedroom.

He went out the back door.

*

When he returned, he came into the bedroom, laid down beside me, and pulled me into his arms.

"I'm sorry," he sobbed. "I'll never do that again."

"I don't want to live like this, Carter," I cried. "I told you how I grew up. I don't want this."

"I promise," he whispered in my ear. I fell asleep in his arms.

*

The next day, he was up and gone for an interview. Hating myself, I laid in bed numb, worried, and scared. After a shower, I took my last ride to the dealership and turned the bike in. It was something I had worked so hard to achieve, so I protected it. I didn't think I deserved it.

"Oh, you're here. Didn't think you were. Where's your bike?" Carter asked when he walked in later that day.

"I turned it in."

"Why would you do that?"

"You're really asking me that?"

"I told you it wouldn't happen again, and I meant it."

At the risk of starting an argument, I kept quiet.

"What are you going to do for a ride now?"

"There's a guy who's getting out with me that I met in transition class. He's selling a beat-up old Tercel for $500."

"You got that kind of cash?"

"I'll figure it out."

Since I was barely scraping by, I sucked it up and called Dad. He knew Paul and I had split and that I had moved on.

"Dad, I'm in a tight spot with money pending my discharge. Could I please borrow $500?" There was no way I could tell him the truth. "I promise to pay you back as soon as I'm released."

"You okay? You've always been good with money." He knew how I ran myself financially. He had taught me.

"Yeah, it's just tight." I wanted to let it out, tell him what was going on and ask for help, but I didn't know how.

"All right, I'll drop a check in the mail. You should have it in a few days. I love you."

"Love you, too. Thanks, Dad." I hung up the phone and sobbed.

*

Walking around outside our apartment complex one day trying to get some exercise, I came across a young stray kitten. She was loving and playful, and some unconditional love sounded good, so I brought her home. Carter didn't argue about her, and we named her Tasha.

Never could I have imagined what such an act of love would eventually turn into.

* * *

After almost five years of military service, life as a civilian began again. I needed to find a job. At a seminar on life after the military, I was advised to look into the legal field because it was better pay than most administrative jobs. Avionics was out.

I kept my eye out for any legal positions for a couple of months and took a few temp jobs. Then an ad showed up for an administrative secretarial position at a small law firm. They were willing to train me as a legal secretary. Putting on a suit, I brought my résumé to them in person and thankfully landed the job.

I began training with a coworker named Maurine—Mo for short. We quickly became friends, and Mo guided me through the procedures, court rules, and all that went with the legal world.

As we got to know one another, we lunched together often and became friends outside of work. Mo was married to a man she'd dated since high school. They seemed like a fun couple who had it all together. They were pregnant with their first child and looking forward to raising a family.

* * *

I was searching for family through friends. But I was always going through the motions, watching other people's happiness and not knowing how to achieve it for myself, trying not to feel doomed and cursed. Smiling on the outside to cover up my misery, I really just wanted to jump off a bridge. I wanted a way out. All I did was go deeper into depression and trouble, afraid and never turning to the only One who could help.

> *So do not fear, for I am with you; do not be dismayed, for I am your God. I will strengthen you and help you; I will uphold you with my righteous right hand.*[4]

* * *

Paul called to check in. It had been months since we spoke, and I got choked up at the sound of his voice.

"You okay?" he asked, concerned.

"Yeah, just had a sneezing fit, so I'm goopy," I lied, trying to gain my composure. "How's everything with you?"

"Good. Found a job, got an apartment. Everything's rolling. How about you?"

"Great." A big fat lie. "I'm out now, too, and found a job I really like."

We chatted, caught up a little, and then Paul said, "Listen, I think we should go ahead and file, get it over with so we can both really move on."

"I think I can take care of it myself. I'll see what it entails and get it done."

It was the last time we spoke. That chapter was closed.

But from the frying pan into the fire I went.

* * *

Carter lost and then found another job. We moved for the second time, and our relationship got back on track.

Just after we settled in, Tasha snuck out, and we got a hard lesson in taking in a stray because she liked to stray. Then she turned up pregnant. Carter handled it well. Hope started creeping in, and I relaxed.

We had a blast watching the kittens grow up, playing on the stairs, wrestling, and then tumbling down. They would look at me like *Whoa! What just happened?* and then dive back into wrestling with each other. When they were old enough for new homes, we gave four of them away and ended up with three.

Once Tasha stopped nursing, she wanted to go on the prowl again. We kept her indoors, but then she started leaving piles of crap at the base of the door and on the windowsills. We realized she was in heat again by the small drop of blood on top of the piles.

*

"I hate that cat. If it doesn't stop, she's out of here," Carter went off about her one day.

"Just have more patience with her. Don't shoo her away and talk mean to her when she loves on you."

We were sitting on opposite ends of the couch, and just as the words left my mouth, Tasha walked over to Carter. I thought he was going to love on her when he picked her up. Instead, he threw her into the side of my head with such force that it just didn't register. All I could do was sit there stunned.

He'd gone from zero to 60 again. He was enraged and just stood there looking at me with fire in his eyes. Tasha ran off, and I knew better than to engage him any further, so I went upstairs.

When the shame set in a bit later, he came to me with his apologies.

11

My brother Todd had graduated, joined the Navy, and was in boot camp.

"I'm coming to California!" he told me excitedly in a phone call just before he graduated. "Will you pick me up at the airport?"

"Of course. When?"

Finally, there was something to look forward to.

*

"Hey, Tsetse Fly."

When she was little, Julie's daughter—Lil's granddaughter—had a hard time saying my name, and it came out Tsetse. Todd used to tease me and call me Tsetse Fly. Only him.

Turning and realizing I'd passed him up, we both started cracking up and ran into each other's arms. He was grown, slim, and trim—a squid.

"Let me see you march," I teased.

"Shut up."

"You look good."

"Yeah, took some weight off." He flashed a huge smile. "I don't have to tell you, but it feels so good to be out of that house."

Wrapping our arms around each other, we made our way through the airport, two survivors still trying to survive.

On the ride to Long Beach, I learned we had each been trapped in our own private hells trying to hang on and claw our way out. I didn't breathe a word to him about what I had going on because I was too embarrassed. I didn't want him to know my path. I didn't want to admit it to myself.

* * *

"That cat is dead!" Carter screamed as he went flying past me, heading downstairs.

Dropping my toothbrush, I ran into the bedroom, saw the pile of bloody poop on his pillow, and instantly panicked that I might die, too. Then Tasha screamed, and I took off downstairs.

He had her by the scruff and was jerking her around talking trash to her.

"Don't hurt her," I begged. "I promise I'll find her another home."

He took her into the bathroom, shoved her in the toilet, and shut the lid.

Then he walked over to me, hit me across the face, and shoved me backward.

"Try to help her!" he screamed.

His rage was so fierce and the look in his eyes so savage that I was terror-struck.

He shoved me up the stairs. I cleaned up the cat's mess and then laid there stiff as a board next to him as I listened to Tasha howl.

Throwing off the covers, he stomped downstairs. Tasha stopped howling, a door slammed, and Carter clomped back upstairs and laid down.

"What'd you do?"

"Took her out but left her in the bathroom."

Watching the sunrise, I said a prayer for Tasha, not even considering myself.

The next morning, Carter was up and gone. He took Tasha with him.

"She's going to the pound," he announced.

* * *

Sitting alone in the car one day, broken and sobbing, I wanted to live but not like I was. Existing on a treadmill of hot coals with a bed of nails at the end is what my life felt like. The patches of grass in between just set me up for another run of pain and letdown.

Not knowing what love was, I hung in with Carter, believing I loved him. Life settled down. We were both working, and our relationship was in a better place—again.

"Thanks for sticking with me, Babe. I'm really sorry for the way I've acted sometimes," Carter said, striking up a conversation one day.

"Thanks for saying that." I was so gullible. "Let's keep moving forward."

"You deserve a good man, and I want to be that for you."

With no idea of my place in life, I believed deep down that there was something better ahead. At the time, I thought the better was Carter's turnaround.

*

We still had three young cats. One of them, named Bear, was Carter's favorite. About a week after Carter took Tasha to the pound, we woke up one morning and couldn't find Bear. It was out of character because all three cats always came running to be fed in the morning. We called for him and looked everywhere, but we found nothing.

Standing in the living room trying to think of where to check next, Carter looked around and said, "Ah crap!" I followed his line of sight.

He had left his Igloo lunch container open on the floor to dry out, like he had done many times. But it was closed, and there was liquid around the bottom of it.

As we got near it, the smell of urine hit us. Carter picked it up and then quickly set it back down.

We cried as he opened it.

Bear had squeezed himself in. Because the lid was sort of cocked against the wall, it shut and locked, suffocating him.

Was it our punishment? Was it Carter's punishment for how he had treated Tasha? Was it my punishment for not scooping up all of them and running out the door?

* * *

During my first year in the service, I had kept in touch with Ted—the brother of Tom's wife, Nancy. (Tom and Nancy had married while I was in boot camp.) But our communication had fizzled. We hadn't spoken since Camp Pendleton. The phone rang one day, and his familiar voice made me duck into the kitchen because Carter was in the living room.

"How are you?" he asked.

"Doing good," I lied. "Surprised to hear from you."

"I know. Tom gave me your number. I'm in town on business and wanted to see if we could get together."

Knowing I'd lose it in front of him, I couldn't. And if Carter found out. . .

"Ah, that sucks. Not that you're in town. . . " I laughed, trying to lighten my lie. "I'm just packing to head to Palm Springs with friends. When are you leaving?"

"Sunday morning. It's okay. Just thought I'd try."

He made it easy for me.

*

A couple days after that, another familiar voice almost dropped me to the floor.

"I'm so glad your number hasn't changed," Steve exclaimed. "How are you?

"Doing good," my voice cracked. "What's going on with you?"

"I'm back home."

We caught each other up on where we were and what we were doing. Of course, I didn't tell him the truth.

"Listen," he said toward the end of our conversation. "I called because I've been thinking about you. I wanted to apologize."

"For what?"

"My behavior toward the end of our relationship. I didn't mean to scare you, and I want you to know I never would've hurt you. It's why we ended. You meant a lot more to me than what I showed you."

Gripping the phone and trying not to lose it, I managed to say, "Thanks for saying that." But what I wanted to say was please come and save me.

The cycle of abuse is an insane ride.

* * *

Was I being shown that better men—flawed but better—had appreciated me?

> I will instruct you and teach you in the way you should go.[1]

The way He shows us isn't always pleasant. It's not the Lord's fault but our choices.

*

Carter came home ecstatic about a new dream job as an apartment complex maintenance man. He told me all about it and then said, "We'll have to move again."

"I'm cool with it."

Then out of the blue, he took me by the hand, led me to the couch, and sat me down.

"I love you so much." His hands were shaking.

"I love you, too."

He seemed nervous, like something was up.

"I've never been this happy."

He slid down off the couch onto a knee and pulled a ring out of his pocket.

"Will you marry me?" Then he gave me that beautiful smile of his.

*

Next was Vegas about a month later with Carter's family and some close friends. It was a fun crew. Everyone flew out together the day before, and we all had a nice dinner that evening.

We married the next day in a small chapel where Carter's parents had once tied the knot. After the ceremony, we all changed clothes to hit the town. Carter stayed back to chat with his parents in their room, and the rest of us waited in the casino in our hotel. About 15 minutes later, Carter came storming toward me across the floor. Instantly, I knew it wasn't going to be good. Crazy was back and headed straight toward me.

"Let's go." He walked up and grabbed my arm.

"No," I pulled away from his grip. "You need to calm down before I'll go anywhere with you."

He snapped and grabbed me by the hair. His fist was clenched, and he pulled with so much force that it made me bend down. He had control and dragged me to a doorway not far from where we were standing.

Not one person came to my aid. In the back seat of life again, I was all by myself with a lunatic driving.

He forced me through the doorway and finally let go of my hair, but I didn't dare say a word.

"Let's go," he demanded, pushing me from behind to climb the stairs in front of us. We reached an area overlooking the city and sat down on a window sill.

"What happened?" I cautiously inquired.

In his fury, his face had contorted into an evil mask. I kept staring out the window.

"My parents," he spewed. "They think they know everything. They wanted to talk to me about responsibility, how lucky I am to have found you and not to mess it up. I hate my dad, so I . . . " He stopped.

"So you what?"

"So I knocked his ass out."

Mortified and scared to death, I sat there with him for a while in silence. Afraid to speak, I was hoping someone would come looking for us and save me.

Of course, his guilt kicked in, and for what seemed like hours, he cried, got mad, and cried again.

"It would be better just to end it," he sobbed. It was his go-to line after outbursts.

We finally headed back to our room and made it through the night, another sleepless one for me.

*

The flight back home the next day was solemn. Everyone who had come with us was on the plane except for Joyce and Norm. Norm was in the hospital with a concussion.

Reflecting out the window, I started waking up on the flight home. The remorse Carter showed after acting out was his way of trying to rein in whatever damage he had caused to see if he could continue the game. He thrived off the conflict he created. His talk of suicide didn't faze me anymore. I was hardened to it.

Staring out the window, all I said was "God . . ." *You weren't supposed to be here, child* was sadly on my mind.

* * *

A couple of weeks later, I went to visit my in-laws. Norm was in bad shape and didn't look good. The force of the punch was so hard that he lost his sense of smell and most of his sense of taste.

"We're concerned for your well-being," he told me.

"Me, too. But I'll figure it out. I've always wanted to ask you guys some questions. Is that okay?"

"Of course," they answered simultaneously.

"When Carter lived with his grandmother, I was under the impression he was helping take care of her. Was that the case?"

"No," Joyce said firmly. "You know he was married before, right?"

"I knew he'd been with someone, but I didn't know whether they were married."

Carter had told me about the relationship, describing a situation very similar to mine with Paul. She had cheated on him at some point, and all went downhill from there.

"He was staying at my mom's," Joyce said, "because he was separated from Melissa and needed a place to stay because no one else would take him in. He's burnt too many bridges. You know about Stephanie, right?"

Stephanie was Carter's daughter with Melissa.

"Yes. He told me about the day he came home and they were gone. He has no idea where they are."

"I don't think he does know. Melissa took Stephanie and got the hell out of there. She's never looked back."

"Do you guys keep in touch with her?"

"No. It's sad because we don't get to see our only grandchild anymore," Norm said sadly. "I don't think she wants us to know because of Carter."

"When did his anger start?"

"He's been an angry, headstrong person since childhood. He always fought direction. He pulled this crap at home, and that's why he doesn't live here. We had a major falling out." Norm shook his head.

"Is that why there are no pictures of him in your house?"

"Yes," Joyce hissed. "I couldn't look at him. We had just begun to try to repair our relationship when you came along. We were hoping you'd be the turnaround, but . . . I'm sorry you're going through this."

"Is there anything we can do to repair all this?" I asked. The thought of being in another broken family killed me.

"We've always wanted him to see a doctor to find out if he has some kind of imbalance going on, but he refuses. Do you think you can get him to go?"

"I can try."

My stomach sank at the thought of approaching him with that.

*

Carter knew I'd gone to visit his parents and asked about it later.

"How'd it go?" He sat down on the other side of the counter.

"Your dad's not good."

He blew out his breath and slouched in the chair.

I cautiously added, "You really need to fix this situation somehow."

"Got any suggestions?"

"You're not going to like it. You've been asked before." Feeling like I wanted to throw up, I held on to the counter. He just looked at me. He knew what was coming.

"Are you willing to see a doctor?" I had to try.

"Is that what you want me to do?"

"I want you to fix the relationship. If that's what it takes, I hope you will."

He nodded his head in agreement.

"It will take time to repair and will eventually work itself out," I encouraged him.

"Come here," he motioned to me with his hands as he stood up.

Walking around the counter, I thought I was going in for a hug. Instead, Carter took me down to the ground before I even knew what happened. He did it gently, kind of jokingly, and I thought he was playing around, lightening the mood. Laughing, I tried to wriggle out of his grip because he was tickling me.

But then he pinned my arms down and dipped his head down. I thought he was going to kiss me, but instead, he tilted his head to the side and bit me hard on the cheek.

I screamed.

He quickly pushed up off of me, and I jumped up, ran into the bedroom, and locked myself in.

*

With an obvious odd-shaped bruise on my cheek, I went to work anyway the next day, not wanting to be at home.

"What the hell happened?" Mo asked when she saw me.

Immediately, I teared up and motioned her to come across the hall to the bathroom.

"He bit me," I cried. I don't remember how much I told her about the mess I was in, but it was a lot.

"You have to get out."

Toward the end of the day, John, one of my bosses, called me into his office. Three of the attorneys I worked for were in there.

"Have a seat," John offered.

"What's going on?"

"Maurine filled us in on your personal life," one of them stated.

No words came, and I just sat there, degraded, with my head down.

Then each one of them started laying into me. I couldn't address their questions fast enough.

"What are you doing with someone like that?"

"Don't you value yourself more than that?"

"Do you enjoy being beat?"

"People won't respect you."

"Do you know how stupid you are?"

They called me stupid! There was no compassion or care in their voices. It was disdain, as if I had committed some terrible crime.

"Look, this is none of your business. It's not something I want to discuss with you."

"We're going to have to let you go," John coldly quipped.

"You're a coward. Don't bother because I quit!"

Rushing out of his office and grabbing my stuff, I left without a word to Mo, but we did make eye contact. She called later that day.

"I'm so sorry."

"I know you were coming from a place of concern."

"What happened in there?"

She got the update.

"What the . . . I had no idea. I meant to help, not cause more grief. I can't say sorry enough. What are you going to do?"

"Find a job first and then figure out the rest."

The story Carter got was that my bosses were pissed off about a mistake I made and let me go. After job hunting, I found a position working for a couple of attorneys on the other side of town.

Then Carter changed jobs, and we moved for the fourth time.

* * *

Carter's brother Chris came to visit one day. The three of us went to have lunch at a joint close to our house. We talked and got caught up on what was going on in each other's lives. Then the topic of their parents came up.

"How's Dad doing?" Carter asked.

"Dude, you . . . " Chris struggled with what he wanted to say. "I can't back you on what you did. There's a point where this has to stop. It's come to that. I don't think the relationship can be repaired."

Carter sighed and then put his chin in his hands.

"Do you want a relationship with Mom and Dad?"

"Yeah, I do."

"Will you go see a doctor then, please?" Thinking it'd be safe with Chris there, I went for it again. Maybe we could get through to him together.

Instead, Carter threw a quick jab to the side of my head, right there in the restaurant. Chris sat there stunned just looking at me. Before the tears could fall, I got up from the table and walked home.

*

Carter showed up a while later. It was almost dusk. I was sitting on the couch when he came into the living room.

"Do you know what happened to that magazine I was reading?" he asked, standing behind me.

"Haven't seen it."

"Did you throw it away? Because you throw everything away."

"Last time I saw it, it was in the bathroom."

"It's not there. You probably threw it."

Dizziness suddenly hit me, and I passed out. Carter had cracked me on the side of the head again and walked off without saying another word. Coming to, alone on the couch, I sobbed into a pillow wishing I had just died.

*

The abuse was escalating. Needing to think, I left for a week and went to visit Dad. Dealing with Lil was better than my own home life. Without much information, Dad knew I was in a situation. My self-worth was void, and I was ashamed. Lying in my former bed one night, I sucked it up, looked out the window, and prayed.

"Lord, it's been a while—a really long while. I'm in a mess, and I don't know what to do."

While crying myself to sleep, I heard this softly impressed in my thoughts: *I'm here, child.*

* * *

Scripture tells us, "Therefore, there is now no condemnation for those who are in Christ Jesus."[2]

* * *

Carter was upbeat when he picked me up at the airport.

"I missed you. I messed up, but I promise, it's going to change."

"It has to, or we're done." It caught his attention, and he turned to look at me. "If you don't go see the doctor, that's it," I said. It was an ultimatum.

"I'll go," he agreed.

We called his parents on the spot so they could make an appointment. But there was no magic pill for his behavior.

* * *

My brother Todd dropped by soon after that.

"I'm being discharged." He had been dealing with his own demons. "Do you think I could move in with you guys, just until I get situated and figure things out?"

He still knew nothing of what I was dealing with. He got along with Carter. We took the idea to him.

"We'll need a bigger place," Carter laughed.

Secretly, I hoped things would be better with Todd around. Was this the answer to my prayer? And it just so happened that a larger apartment next door to us would be coming vacant soon.

It was part of the answer to my prayer but not the way I thought.

*

In the meantime, Dad was worried about us both. He called one night.

"Would it be all right if I came for a visit?" he asked.

"Of course. I'm excited for you to come."

Carter was fine with it—at the time.

*

Dad flew out that summer and rented a car. We planned on him staying with us, but Carter went on a bizarre tirade from the get-go.

"I don't want someone like you in our house!" he screamed as Dad, Todd, and I walked in.

The three of us froze. Dad played it cool.

"I don't mean to impose," Dad said. "I just want to see my kids. I'll stay in a hotel, no problem. I don't want to cause any problems."

I was ashamed. While walking Dad and Todd back to the car, I was secretly relieved, afraid for Dad to be around Carter.

"Don't say anything to him. It's fine. Just stay safe," Dad whispered as he hugged me goodbye. As I turned to walk back in, I saw Carter waving from the balcony.

* * *

Dad came over while Carter was at work. He went through the paper with Todd and taught him how to job hunt and prepare for interviews. He even took him to some of the locations once Todd was contacted by potential employers.

"What's Lil been up to?" I asked when we finally had time to sit, relax, and talk. "You haven't said anything about her. Is she missing you?"

He took a slow, deep breath like he was taking a moment to think about what he was going to say.

"Lil's going to be moving back to Pennsylvania. I'm not going with her."

"What? Finally!" I exclaimed.

"No way," Todd added.

"Once you kids were gone, I realized I don't want to live like that anymore. I'd rather be on my own. When she told me she wanted to start slowing down and move nearer to her family, I started making different plans. She wanted me to go with her, but the thought of being around more people like her wasn't appealing. She doesn't know yet, but I've already found a little house. I'll be moving out when I get back."

We celebrated.

The floodgates opened, and Dad got emotional.

"I failed you kids in many ways by not teaching you the proper tools to go out into life with. I recognize you're both struggling. I'm sorry and want you both to know that."

We went for it all, unloading our feelings and anger about the way he treated us when we were growing up and what a jerk we thought he was. We cried together.

Dad turned to address me directly. "I'm proud of you. I know you're smarter than the situation you're in. You need to get out of it."

"You're right. I'm at that point. I just need the right opening, and I'll take it," I bawled.

"Do you need help with money?"

"No. This is something I need to figure out and take care of myself."

He turned to Todd. "Help your sister if she needs it. Support her."

"I will," Todd promised.

It was bittersweet saying goodbye when Dad left. But the three of us were in a much better place even though our lives were separately imploding. Feeling stronger, I began praying.

Just after Dad left, Todd landed a job.

* * *

Forgiveness is everything, the key to unlocking it all.

> *For if you forgive other people when they sin against you, your heavenly Father will also forgive you. But if you do not forgive others their sins, your Father will not forgive your sins.*[3]

The Lord knows when forgiveness is really in our hearts—when we let go.

He will not always accuse, nor will he harbor his anger forever; he does not treat us as our sins deserve or repay us according to our iniquities. For as high as the heavens are above the earth, so great is his love for those who fear him; as far as the east is from the west, so far has he removed our transgressions from us. As a father has compassion on his children, so the LORD *has compassion on those who fear him; for he knows how we are formed, he remembers that we are dust.*[4]

12

Todd worked graveyard and was gone most weekends. About a month had gone by when we ran into each other just as he was heading out for work. We chatted for a few minutes, and then his tone turned serious.

"I have to tell you something."

"What's up?"

"Yesterday I walked into the kitchen, and Carter was there. He didn't hear me coming, so he kind of jumped in surprise and tried to hide what he was doing, but I saw it." He paused.

"What?"

"He was warming up meth in the microwave."

I didn't know a lot about meth, but what I did know hit me like a freight train. Understanding came into focus about the roller coaster ride that wouldn't stop. Opening up, I told Todd about what had been going on.

"I've seen it in you guys. I was there when he went off on Dad, remember? You have to get out of this."

"I know."

*

The next day I spoke to Carter.

"He's a liar. It was just a snack," Carter yelled.

Knowing he'd never tell me the truth, I just wanted to see his reaction.

"You can't hide the lie anymore. Unless you get help, we're done."

"Oh, we're done because you say we are? What am I going to get help for, heating up food? Piss off."

"Figure out somewhere to go, Carter. I don't want you here anymore."

"You've got Toddy now, so I'm roadkill. This is my place, too," he said, childlike.

"Don't think you can rely on me anymore. I'm done carrying you." I left before anything else could break out.

Distancing myself as much as I could, I opened my own bank account but kept it to myself. In rebellion for my being gone more often, Carter started having parties all the time. Strange people were in the apartment, and who knows what else was going on, but the scene wasn't good.

He was putzing around in the garage one evening when I got home.

"Have you made any plans for a new place?" I asked.

"I'm good with the one I've got," he said as he lit a cigarette. "How 'bout you? You're Miss Whatever lately. What're your plans?"

"We have separate bank accounts now." It was matter-of-fact. "So you'll need to take care of whatever." Popping my hip, I took the same stance as he had when he said, "Miss Whatever."

"I hate you," he stepped forward and screamed in my face, blowing out smoke.

"I'm done," I yelled back. "I want you to leave."

"You're giving up. You're psychotic like your mom." Then he started calling me every name in the book.

"Your words can't hurt me anymore. You can't hurt me anymore. I'm already gone."

His anger rose more, and his face started contorting. He flicked the cigarette he'd been smoking at my face, so I went up to the apartment.

A few minutes later, he was right behind me. Coming at me, he forced me back into the wall, punching me in the ribs and then throwing me across the room.

"Get out," I yelled, but he had me by my arm and continued punching.

Swirling out of his grasp, I ran into the bedroom, locked the door, and called the police while he screamed and banged on the door.

"The cops are on their way," I yelled.

He went silent.

It took about 20 minutes for the police to get there. I had already come out of the bedroom, walked past Carter, and gone outside to sit on the steps with a mess of scratches and bruising already appearing.

"Lord, what do I do?" I prayed.

Two officers showed up. As they were walking up the steps toward me, one of them asked, "Where is he?"

"Inside," I thumbed to the door. The officer stepped past me and knocked.

As the second officer approached, he looked me over and asked, "What'd you do to piss him off?"

What? I screamed in my head. Deflated, I started crying, told him about the argument, and gave him a brief history of Carter's violence.

He didn't respond but just stepped past me and went into the apartment.

Standing in the doorway, I listened.

"She's crazy. Mental illness runs in her family. You should be carting her off," Carter tried to convince the officers.

"Listen, we need you to settle down," one of them said. "Are there any drugs in the house?"

"No. See, she's trying to turn this around on me."

"Look, we either take you in or you can leave for the night. We can't allow you to stay here."

They waited as he gathered some things. The officer that talked to me on the steps accompanied Carter to his car. As they passed me, he told Carter, "Hey man, don't let her take you there."

The other officer addressed me. "If you're serious about getting out, you should get a restraining order. He's pretty hopped up. We'll make sure he doesn't come back tonight."

*

Alone, battered, and bruised, I laid down to rest and reached out to God. "Lord, I need help. It's hit the fan down here. Please, I don't know what else to do."

As I lay there sobbing in the silence, softly but firmly I was told, "Get out."

* * *

The next day, I stayed home from work waiting to talk to Todd. With barely a word out of my mouth, Todd politely cut me off.

"I'm not living like this anymore or watching you live like this," Todd stated. "I'm thinking about moving in with a friend of mine."

"Would you be my roommate instead? I'll go in for a restraining order to cover both of us and find us a new place. We'll get the hell out of here."

"Let's do it."

We sealed it with a hug and made a plan.

Our landlord was cool and didn't want a situation, so he accepted our notice to move out of the apartment with only five days left in the month and didn't charge us a penalty. We scheduled turn-offs with all the utility companies. Next was an apartment. I found one on the other side of town. Todd went with me, and we were able to secure the place on the spot. Then we reserved a moving van.

*

At work the next day, I filled in my employers on what was going on. They encouraged what I was doing and allowed me to prepare the paperwork for the restraining order. Then I gave Carter notice about court the next morning.

Worried about the animals, I returned to the old apartment, but Carter was there. The place was in shambles. He had gone through all my stuff.

"I need to get some things from the bedroom."

"No, you're not going in there. The cats are in there."

"The police can assist me."

That got his attention, and he opened the bedroom, trailing behind me the entire time. The animals were okay.

"If you do anything to harm them, I'll have you arrested," I threatened while grabbing what I needed.

Driving off, I said a prayer for the safety of the animals.

*

Carter didn't attend the hearing, so he was served with the order at his work. Then I dropped off a copy to the police department. They told me to call if I needed assistance.

Todd took the day off and was waiting with the moving truck so we'd be ready to go. It was getting late into the afternoon, and we only had about a two-hour window to get done and be gone.

There were only two of us, but it felt like 10 because we packed up and loaded the truck like the place was on fire. Determined and focused on our task, we barely spoke. Several neighbors came out to be nosy, but no one asked if they could lend a hand.

The last to go were the animals. As soon as we started pulling out of the alleyway, along came Carter. I kept going, and Todd followed behind me in the truck.

As we got out onto the main street, we realized Carter was following us. Not wanting him to find out where we were going, I motioned out the window for Todd to pull up alongside me. I yelled, "Follow me" and then headed for the police station.

It worked! As we got closer, Carter figured it out and dropped out of sight.

We made it to our new place safe and sound. We were exhausted, but we unpacked the truck anyway. We were free!

Almost. . .

*

About a week later, Todd called me at work.

"You okay?" He sounded worried.

"Yeah, what's wrong? You okay?"

"I am. My car's not. When I went to leave this morning, all my tires were slashed."

"You're kidding! Did anyone see anything?"

"No. It gets better. I parked in an area where the cameras don't work."

"Oh no! Need me to come get you?"

"I'm good. The service is already here changing them."

"All right. Make sure you park in a well-lit area or find out where the cameras are and park there."

"Already figured that out. See you later."

We knew who did it, but there was nothing we could do about it.

*

After that I got served at work with divorce papers. Then Carter called.

"You got the papers?"

"Yeah. I would've taken care of it."

"I wanted to beat you to the punch so you could feel what it's like to be served at work."

*

After our divorce proceedings commenced, I went to visit Mo. The last time we'd gotten together, something was off. She finally opened up, and we realized we had even more in common. Her marriage was falling apart, too.

When I left her place and got down to my car, everything was all wrong. My car wasn't where I had parked it. It had rolled down the street several yards and hit a vehicle. The front end of my car was smashed, and the other car had a scratch. The owner was cool

164

about the situation, and nothing came of it except the damage to my vehicle.

As I was getting out of my car at home, Carter came rolling up in a vehicle I didn't recognize—a red Chevy van. It hadn't taken him long to figure out where we lived.

"What're you doing here?"

"I don't know," he scratched his head dramatically. "Had a funny feeling something happened to you." Then he over-exaggerated when he saw the front end of my car.

"What happened?"

It was his worst acting performance since I'd met him.

"Give me my key back immediately or I'm calling the cops."

He hesitated and then reached into his pocket and handed me the key.

"Hey, I didn't have anything to do with it. You must not have put on the emergency brake," he shrugged and then laughed.

"Leave, or I'm calling the cops."

As I walked up the stairs, he drove off, but chills went up my spine when I realized he had followed me.

It pissed me off that I was scared again.

* * *

Todd had car trouble one day—nothing related to Carter. We were trying to figure it out when a tall, slim man came walking up. He was rough looking, and just by his demeanor, we could tell he was an addict or had been.

"Hi, I'm Joe," he introduced himself. "Need any help? I'm pretty good with cars."

"Yes," we collectively gasped.

While he was working, we got to talking.

"You new to the place?" Todd asked.

"I've been around," Joe told us. "My parents live in the upstairs apartment behind the garages. I'm staying with them for a little while." Then he told Todd, "Try it now."

The car still sounded like crap.

"I know what it is!" Joe exclaimed. "Need the right tool. Follow me."

He led us a couple of doors down.

"This is my parents' garage," he told us as he lifted the door.

"Holy crap," Todd cried.

It was packed full inside. Joe had to tunnel through to get around.

"Ah! Found it!" He came flying back out of the maze all happy. "Now we'll get it done."

"So, do you work?" I asked.

"Nobody will hire me," he pointed at his eye, which was scarred shut.

"What happened?" Todd asked.

"My sister shot it out with a BB gun when we were kids. It was rough after that. Got into drugs. I've lived on the streets most of my life, collecting and trading things. Had a meth addiction, and I've been trying to kick it again."

He straightened up from being under the hood.

"Don't ever mess with the stuff," he pointed at us.

"No, thank you," I said. "We've already experienced some of its side effects, indirectly."

It was cryptic, but he caught on.

"That the guy I've seen come around here in the van?" he one-eyed me intuitively.

"Yeah."

"Just yell if you ever need to. I know how to handle jackholes like that." He looked me in the eyes. "Don't hesitate."

"Thanks." It was nice. Comforting.

"Try it now," he directed Todd, and the car sounded great.

*

A couple weeks later, I ran into Joe, and he introduced me to his parents, Papa Joe and Nina. They were up in years, late 60s. Papa Joe was crippled with arthritis but was still an upbeat, positive person.

"It's nice to meet you, young lady." He shook my hand but didn't let go.

"Nice to meet you, too."

"I understand Joe was able to help you and your brother out." He still had quite a grip on my hand.

"He did. We owe him one."

"You don't owe me nothin'," Joe said.

"That was God watching out for you, child." Papa Joe loosened his grip, looked me in the eyes, and asked, "Will you come and talk with me sometime?"

"I'd love to."

*

We took to each other right off the bat. Growing more comfortable, we shared stories. Without telling him much, he understood I'd gotten myself out of a bad situation.

"Is that what happened to your car?" Papa Joe asked over his glasses.

"Yes, it had something to do with it."

It wasn't hard to tell where Joe got his intuition.

"What about your faith?"

"My . . . I . . . " I didn't know what to say.

He looked at me intently with his blue eyes and waited.

Sharing my experience with church, I explained that I hadn't been back since. "I still believe, but . . . I go through rough patches with it. Really, my belief is a rough patch." Opening up to him about some of my childhood, I explained how I felt forgotten, doomed.

Papa Joe cried.

"Wait here." He struggled out of his chair and returned, carrying his Bible. "Let me show you through scripture who you are."

My eyes opened, and I began to understand the peaceful, forgiving, and awarding side of God. What I had thought were harshness and punishment were really lessons of guidance and discipline.

During my next visit, Papa Joe and Nina gave me a Bible.

God met me more than halfway, he freed me from my anxious fears. Look at him; give him your warmest smile. Never hide your feelings from him. When I was desperate, I called out, and God got me out of a tight spot.[1]

If we admit our sins—make a clean break of them—he won't let us down; he'll be true to himself. He'll forgive our sins and purge us of all wrongdoing. If we claim that we've never sinned, we out-and-out contradict God—make a liar out of him. A claim like that only shows off our ignorance of God.[2]

Make this your common practice: Confess your sins to each other and pray for each other so that you can live together whole and healed. The prayer of a person living right with God is something powerful to be reckoned with. Elijah, for instance, human just like us, prayed hard that it wouldn't rain, and it didn't—not a drop for three and a half years. Then he prayed that it would rain, and it did. The showers came and everything started growing again. My dear friends, if you know people who have wandered off from God's truth, don't write them off. Go after them. Get them back and you will have rescued precious lives from destruction and prevented an epidemic of wandering away from God.[3]

* * *

Car troubles began plaguing me.

"What're you going to do?" Papa Joe asked.

"Don't know. I'm going to have to start looking around. Can't afford a new car. Hopefully a decent used one will come my way."

"Well, let's sit down and think about this." He took out a pad of paper and grabbed a pen. "What can you budget monthly for a payment?"

"Probably around $200 because insurance still has to be factored in."

He ran some numbers on a calculator.

"If I can get you into a new car for that kind of payment with a trade-in, would you do it?"

"You can do that?"

"I told you what I used to do for a living, right?"

"You did. It must not have registered."

"Cars, baby," he exclaimed. "I owned a dealership."

*

Within a week, Papa Joe found an advertisement for a deal at a local dealership. A couple hours after we walked in, I drove out with a brand new '92 Mustang. They didn't want my hunk of junk, but Papa Joe kept at the young salesman until he broke and got the payment down to $205.

"I can't thank you enough. Please let me cook dinner for you and Nina tonight."

"No. Don't go to all that trouble."

"It's not trouble. I want to. You've both done so much for me. The best thing I've got is a home-cooked meal. Do you think I can sell this hunk of junk?"

"Is that what you're going to do with the hunk of junk, as you call it?"

"Yeah. If it doesn't sell, I'll see if a scrap yard wants it, I guess."

"Tell you what," he clapped his hands. "I'll take the junk off your hands. If Joey can't fix it, I'll have someone else take a look at it and then sell it and keep the profit."

His offer made me cry.

"Well, I didn't mean to make you cry," he laughed.

"They're tears of joy 'cuz you're just doing me another favor."

As it turned out, the car had a cracked block. Papa Joe didn't make much profit and ended up selling it for parts.

Making arrangements with Nina, I surprised Papa Joe with dinner one night.

> *You use steel to sharpen steel, and one friend sharpens another.*[4]

What Papa Joe did for me was immeasurable. God put him in my life at the right time.

> *It's better to have a partner than go it alone. Share the work, share the wealth. And if one falls down, the other helps. But if there's no one to help, tough! Two in a bed warm each other. Alone, you shiver all night. By yourself you're unprotected. With a friend you can face the worst. Can you round up a third? A three-stranded rope isn't easily snapped.*[5]

* * *

Carter had been leaving Todd alone but stalking me. Sometimes, I'd find him lurking near our apartment. Our unit was toward the back of the complex, and there was a short brick wall that separated the property from a strip mall, so he had easy access to approach from different angles. He'd follow me when I was on a walk or coming and going from work.

A friend's dog had puppies, a gorgeous mix of Labrador and Doberman. Carter was afraid of dogs. Todd and I discussed it and brought home a girl. We named her Coco. I was overjoyed, and she went everywhere with me. She became my walking companion—really my companion for everything—and my best friend.

One evening, Coco and I headed out for a walk when she suddenly stopped in her tracks and began growling a deep, throaty growl. All the hairs on her back went up, her stance was in high alert, and she went into a wild warning bark.

Carter was there hiding in the shadows of the garages. I never even saw him until Coco scared him and he ran.

* * *

I woke up screaming one night, and Todd came running in.

"What's wrong?" he asked.

Sitting up, drenched in sweat, I patted myself down for wounds.

"What're you doing?" He looked panicked.

"It was so real," I mumbled, trying to make sense of the nightmare.

"What was?"

"Remember the movie *The Howling*?"

"Yeah."

"I had a nightmare that Carter was Eddie. He turned into a wolf and then came after me. It was like I was there. I could smell him."

"Did you kill him?"

"No, freak. I was running for my life."

"Don't run next time. Kill him," Todd said jokingly as he headed back to bed.

The nightmare haunted me for weeks, coming back almost nightly with different acts playing out each time. But the end game was always the same. Carter would get mad about something, start mishandling me, and then morph into a mad dog chasing me through whatever scene we were in.

*

At the swap meet with a friend one day, Susan stopped at a booth and exclaimed, "Bet one of these will chase that nightmare away!"

"What is it?"

"A dream catcher.[6] In Indian lore, it's supposed to protect you from bad dreams. It catches them."

"Really?"

"True story. Ask the guy," she pointed.

"She pretty much summed it up," the clerk said and then gave us a bit of a history lesson. At the end, he added, "It helped me when I was having nightmares."

Not even thinking about what I was doing, I hung the catcher above my bed as the clerk had instructed. I may have even said a prayer over it, hoping the nightmare would stop.

But that night, I dreamed that I woke up in our old apartment. It was a mess—furniture toppled, broken glass, stuff everywhere. I was looking for something. Scared and in a hurry, my eye caught a glint of light reflecting across the room. Creeping silently over to it, I hoped it was the box that held the key. But I didn't know why I needed the key.

Something in the distance crashed and sent me looking for cover. There was no time to run. Someone screamed. It sounded like thunder growing from a distance. I could feel his rage. The closet door imploded. I stood in the corner with my back to him. Maybe if I couldn't see the Carter Wolf, it wouldn't be there because this time I was trapped.

"Turn to me," he growled, breathing heavily.

As I turned to face the monster, I opened the box and pulled out Terry's cross.

The wolf screamed in my face, intimidating me with his fangs and slapping a claw against the doorframe. The room shook, making the cross on the opposite wall fall slowly. Watching it, I thought it looked weird, as if moving through honey.

The wolf launched at me.

I jolted upright, drenched in sweat.

The dream catcher had fallen and was lying next to me.

Looking up, I whispered, "Okay, God. I get it."

No other gods, only me. No carved gods of any size, shape, or form of anything whatever, whether of things that fly or walk or swim. Don't bow down to them and don't serve them because I am GOD, your God, and

*I'm a most jealous God, punishing the children for any
sins their parents pass on to them to the third, and yes,
even to the fourth generations of those who hate me.
But I'm unswervingly loyal to the thousands who love
me and keep my commandments.*[7]

Therefore, my dear friends, flee from idolatry.[8]

* * *

"I'm just calling to say goodbye," Carter said the Saturday after
receiving our divorce judgment. I'm headed north. Is it okay if I
swing by?"

"All right." Curious, I wanted to find out what was up.

"Hop in. Let's ride and find a place to talk," he invited sadly.

There is no explanation for why I stepped into that sinister
red van . . .

He was very solemn, like the state he'd been in after clobbering
his dad. Never knowing whether his depression was true or just a
really good acting job, I was just thankful not to have to deal with
it anymore.

"Can't believe we're really divorced," Carter broke the silence.
"It feels like I've lost my best friend."

I was never his best friend, but I didn't add fuel by saying
anything stupid.

"Here, let's go in here," he pointed and then turned into a park.
"Ya know," he cut the engine and sat back in his seat, "you were
smart to get Coco. She scared the crap out of me."

Not sure whether he was trying to bait me, I couldn't help
responding. "There's a reason for her." It was direct and eye-to-eye.

"Understood, but I really thought you were the one."

Carter sat up and began shuffling stuff around in the console
like he was looking for something. As I watched, he exposed a small
revolver. He acted nonchalant, as if he hadn't seen it.

On high alert, I didn't have time to think about how stupid I was to be in this position, but the thought was there. My prayer was silent and quick.

Carter sat up straight without taking anything from the console and covered up the revolver. Looking around the crowded park, I thought about what his intent might be. Did he want to harm me or himself? Or was this another game?

"What are your plans? Where are you relocating?" Keep him talking, I decided.

"I've been learning computer graphics," he perked up. "Been looking around in different areas and found a job in Tahoe. I'm leaving either Tuesday or Wednesday."

"Did you already apply?"

"Yeah, oh yeah. I've got the job."

"Are you looking forward to it?"

"I am," he paused and then added, "Wish you were coming with me."

"We tried that, remember?"

"Wish I had another chance." He tried, even pulling out the puppy dog eyes.

We'd been parked for about 10 minutes. It was time to go.

"So, listen," I said. "Friends are coming over. We're going out tonight, and they'll be waiting on me." It was a lie. He started to say something but instead fired up the van, and we drove back in silence.

"This is goodbye," he said as I jumped out.

"Take care of yourself." Kissing his cheek, I walked away silently, thanking God for keeping me safe.

*

A letter arrived about a month later postmarked from Tahoe. Carter wrote to tell me again how much he missed me.

He got no response.

13

It was time to reflect and figure things out, I told myself. But instead of putting out the Bible Papa Joe and Nina gave me to use, it was stored in a box in the garage. My prayer life was more frequent but not what it should be—more like a daughter who left home and checked in sporadically, depending on what was going on.

> *These people honor me with their lips, but their hearts are far from me.*[1]

* * *

Todd switched to working days, and we hung out a lot, took weekend trips together, and enjoyed hiking and going to concerts. We spoke to Dad several times a week, and both of us valued his life advice, especially through our move and job changes. We enjoyed laughing together at past mistakes and rejoiced in the learning and how far we'd each come. God's loving hand was at work in us.

Dad eventually came to visit. He and Lil had gone their separate ways, and their divorce was final. It was the happiest we'd seen him in a long time. He was such a changed man. There were times when he'd grow sad over regrets, but he had a way of throwing his shoulders back and shaking it off. Now that makes me wonder what his prayer life was like. The three of us were battled-scarred and wounded, but the healing had trumped it all.

*

A few months after Dad's visit, Todd sparked up a conversation.

"You ever think about going back home?" he asked.

"Never. Are you talking Jamestown?"

"Or in the vicinity, like Buffalo or Rochester."

"No. Why? Are you?"

"Been thinking about it. It'd be nice to be closer to Dad. Would you go back if I did?"

"I'd have to think about that one."

It wasn't even something on my radar. During Dad's visit, Todd and I had talked about Dad moving to California to be with us. Dad considered it at first and then said no, that he'd love to be closer but wouldn't be happy in California.

The anguish of Todd's question beat me up for a week, and I avoided him so we wouldn't have to talk about it. Dad's words kept ringing in my head along with the reasons I'd made the escape in the first place. But the thought of having to say goodbye to my brother was like burning acid in my gut. Finally, it had to stop, so one night I stood in the doorway of his bedroom.

"You're on your own," I said.

He stopped typing and looked up at me.

"I've thought about it nonstop all week. I wouldn't be happy going back. If it's time for you to make a change, you have my blessing. Dad's getting to the point where he's going to need one of us around, so maybe it would be a good thing."

The look of hurt that came over his face said it all. Now the misery of the decision was in his court.

*

Watching Todd drive off with all his stuff a few months later almost killed me. My heart felt like it was going to stop. The strength we had helped each other build in our respective lives and the bond between us was unbreakable. But we both knew it was time to go our separate ways.

With the help of friends, I was able to buy my first place a little over a year later. My realtor was Papa Joe's son-in-law, Woody.

*

Just after buying a condo, I met a gal named Monica. She and I worked together and became good friends. Not wanting to risk our friendship, I fought Monica on introducing me to her brother, but she lovingly tricked us both by way of separate invites to a Labor Day celebration. When Mike rolled up in a bikini top red Jeep, it was obvious who he was because he had the same spectacular, beaming smile as his sister. My nerves jumped.

More people arrived, including Michelle and Vern, another sister and her husband. We all took off walking to the Orange County Street Fair. Eventually, the men in the group broke off and headed for a bar while the rest of us walked around. As we walked, Michelle and Monica shared stories about their upbringings. Their dad had been career Army with two tours in Vietnam. We were raised in very similar battles, just different wars.

When the men caught up with us about an hour later, the laughter ensued. But within an hour, the fun took an odd turn. As we all headed back to Monica's, Michelle and I were walking together, getting to know one another, when Vern called out to her from behind us.

"What're you walking with her for?" he yelled out in a slur, drunk. "Come back here with me."

"Just ignore him," she leaned into me and whispered. "He's just kidding around."

But that set him off.

"What are you? Two lesbians now?" he screamed.

"Have you lost your mind?" Michelle turned around to him, and everyone froze in their tracks. We all just stood there for a few seconds in some strange moment.

Then Vern brought us out of it by letting some nasty sewage fly out of his pie hole as he stormed past Michelle and me. We all looked at each other and then started walking again, only in silence. It felt like I had glue stuck to my feet.

By the time everyone reached the main corner, Vern was out of sight. As we stood there waiting for the light to change, the squeal of tires brought us out of our stupor as a car went flying by. It was Vern in some drunken rage he had made up in his own mind. Our heads collectively followed the car as it shot by, and then there was sobbing. Michelle lost it.

Once we reached Monica's house, I quickly used the restroom, said a quick goodbye, and headed for the door. Mike tried to ask me if I wanted to have a drink with him, but I bowed out and left, just wanting to escape the scene.

*

A few weeks later, Mike invited me to a Halloween party, and we've been inseparable ever since. We took our relationship slowly, sharing little by little the experiences that had shaped us so far—two broken people trying to figure it out. Monica had told me about Ryan, but I waited for Mike to tell me about his son when he was ready.

We'd been seeing each other for two months. One day I was telling Mike about an upcoming trip I was taking to see Dad and Todd back in Jamestown for Thanksgiving when he just nervously blurted out that he had a kid.

"You know I have a son, right? Ryan."

"Monica let me know."

"What else did my sister tell you?"

"That it's not so copacetic with his mom." It was a polite paraphrase. The relationship hadn't worked out, they never married, and they had been co-parenting for three years.

"That's not what she said," he laughed.

"No, but I get it. We all have messes."

"Well, I don't mean this in a bad way, but it's kind of good you're going out of town. Ryan's coming, and we haven't discussed all that."

*

Three months later, I was pretty sure Mike was the man of my prayers. It was Valentine's Day.

"Come with me." He took me by the hand and led me into another room.

"For you." He handed me a plant. "This is not just any plant. It's a Bonsai[2] and takes extra love, nurturing, and care to grow, an example for how we should treat our relationship."

The sincerity he said it with and the way he looked at me were everything on this earth and everything ever since.

*

That Easter, Kohl, my Black Lab at the time, busted through Mike's apartment door as I was trying to open it. Ryan was standing in the living room in just his underwear, holding a stuffed rabbit. Kohl tromped up to him, smelled the toy, and then gave Ryan a full-tongue, sloshy lick across the face. Ryan screamed and ran through the kitchen into the TV room as we followed. He jumped into his dad's lap. The happy smile on Mike's face said it all.

That Christmas while we attended a play Ryan was in, Mike and I discussed faith for the first time. We had shared about some of our respective upbringings and recognized that the tests of our faith were very similar.

We knew each other as struggling believers.

*

After dating for three years, we moved in together. There were many trials. The first one wasn't our own, but we watched it from afar along with most of the world as it played out one September morning. I was listening to the news while getting ready for work when the report came of a second plane, and I woke up Mike.

"Babe, watch the TV."

"What's wrong?" He looked up, groggy and squinting with one eye. "What's that?"

"One of the Twin Towers. A plane hit it. They're saying another plane's coming."

We watched together in horror as the attack played out.

Our siblings were going through their own drama. And custody and care issues plagued us as Ryan's mom moved back and forth, state to state. Past relationship concerns between his mom's side of the family got tense, really tense. It was stressful and expensive.

Dad battled lung cancer and lost. It had been a courageous two-year fight. Mike and I got to visit him a couple months before he passed. The cough that racked Dad's frail body in the end sounded like a wounded freight train limping along on broken tracks. Saying goodbye, I knew it would be the last in-person goodbye. I spoke with Dad the morning he went to the Lord. The last thing he said was "I love you."

Mike got in hot water with the IRS for back taxes. Come to find out, his accountant hadn't filed his taxes for six or seven years. It was a mess, and it took almost three years to get it cleared up. Worse yet, it became a family issue, and the fallout lasted another eight or nine years before healing could begin.

Landing in the hospital with a virus, I was diagnosed with migraines after telling the doctors about the intense head pain I'd been having.

Then domestic violence reared its ugly head—not in our camp but in Ryan's.

We had him for the summer and enrolled him in day camp. As I picked him up one day, a counselor pulled me aside.

"We had an issue today." She looked solemn, so she had my attention. "Ryan got in trouble for throwing sand in another kid's face. When I disciplined him, he refused to listen and wouldn't come out of the sandbox. The second time I asked, he yelled at me, told me no, and said to shut up."

My gaze went to Ryan who was standing there looking sheepishly defiant.

"What's up with that?"

"I don't know."

"Not an acceptable answer. You'd better dig a little deeper."

He just stood there.

"We'll get this sorted out," I addressed the counselor. "Sorry you had to deal with his attitude."

She was so bummed, she just turned and walked away.

Holding his hand, I walked him to the car.

"You need to find your words on the ride home. You've got a couple minutes to think about it."

Three blocks later, I turned down the radio.

"What happened?"

We made eye contact quickly, and he blew out a breath.

"I just got mad."

"That's not cool. Where's mad coming from? I've never seen you act like that."

He kept his eyes forward.

"I'm aware of some of the things going on at home."

He turned to look at me.

"Your grandparents talked to your dad and me about it. Would you please tell me so I can hear it in your words?"

His gaze went back to the window. A few minutes went by while he fidgeted in his seat.

"My mom and stepdad are always fighting. Before coming here, they got in a fight—about me. Don was screaming at my mom, calling me a spoiled kid. He kept pushing her. I was screaming at him, trying to help her. Then he forced us into the basement and locked us in."

Turning back to look at me, the hurt was in his eyes, anger on his face. The picture of this eight-year old boy trying to help fend off his stepdad just . . .

It took me a few minutes.

"I'm sorry you're going through that crap. It's not fair, but it's life. You have to find a way to deal with it better and not go down the same path."

"You don't get it."

"Unfortunately . . ."

After sharing some, the anger in his face lightened.

"Your mom has got some stuff to figure out. In the meantime, when you get mad, tap into your self-control and learn to calm down. Walk away from a situation if you have to. There's a better way to live than what you're experiencing."

He nodded his head in understanding.

Mike handled it much the same. His emotions reeled as he tried to control his frustration.

Ryan's eyes were sad when he looked at us. "You guys never fight."

"We do!" we exclaimed together.

"We try to live by the same advice we're giving you," his dad told him.

We worked to break the silence we had each been raised in by having open communication with Ryan. We tried to balance the line between adult and parent-child conversation and came out the other side stronger.

It grew our faith. We began telling each other things like, "Say your prayers," "There's a reason for that, and only God knows," or "God works in mysterious ways."

Mike and I started talking marriage.

* * *

It was a day of extra celebration because the tax issue was settled. It had been seven years since we met. We headed out to the Street Fair. It was a tradition every year. Starving, we searched for our favorite taco stand on Mexican Street and then settled on a curb and chowed down. Mike was lollygagging and fiddling with something, so I stood up to look around and scope out our next stop.

"Let's roll," I urged.

"Hold up. What's your hurry? I'm not done yet. Sit back down."

I'm pretty sure he received some attitude from me, but I sat down.

"Geez, hold on a sec. Check this out," he said.

Still scanning the food selections, I turned to him. He was holding a black velvet box flat in his palm. Then he flashed his cheesiest smile.

All I could do was squint at him.

"What?" The corners of his smile kept twitching. He opened the box.

Opening my eyes in shock and then squinting again, I asked, "Is this for real?"

"No cubic zirconia here!"

"No, I mean how . . . you just settled and . . . "

"Traci," he said sternly so I'd shut up, "will you marry me? Please?"

* * *

A year later, we were barefoot in the sand walking hand-in-hand, and the way he looked at me was still everything. His smile was proud. We said our vows under swaying palm trees with the frothy ebb and flow of water and sand providing background music. The morning clouds were still dissipating, and the beams of light were breaking through over a jetty giving a spectacular display of God's glory.

As we turned to look out over the ocean, we knew possibilities were endless.

* * *

You might think we'd have it down after being together eight years before getting married, but it's been the toughest test of all. The battle over Ryan ensued. We had just gotten home from our honeymoon. We hadn't seen Ryan for a year, ever since he moved out of state again. Ryan caught sight of his dad when he got off the plane and ran into his arms, crying.

"I thought I was never going to get to see you again," he sobbed.

Everyone in the vicinity got choked up.

During the ride home, Ryan fired off questions.

"Why did it take so long for me to come?"

"We're dealing with some things with your mom, and it took some time," Mike told him.

"Mom said you didn't want me to visit anymore."

"That's not true," we said simultaneously.

"Look," Mike took over, "your mom decided to leave again. I had to go to court—again—to be able to see you."

Ryan nodded his head in understanding. It's what he wanted, the truth.

"I know about it," he informed us.

"How's that?"

"It's all mom and grandma talk about. Dad, why can't I come live with you and visit Mom instead?"

"Buddy, we've tried. It's not going to happen. Right now, we just want to see you more."

*

It was his junior year in high school, and we were praying he'd graduate. Things didn't get any easier for Ryan. We supported him the best we could from nearly a thousand miles away. His rebellious stage was a clear indication of the frustration of his upbringing. Midyear, he came for a visit. While cooking dinner one night, he struck up a conversation.

"I have to tell you guys something, but promise not to get mad."

"What's up?"

We braced for impact.

"I'm not living at home anymore. I moved out."

"You're okay though?" Mike took on the conversation.

"Way better."

"Where are you living?"

"With a couple of buddies and their mom right now until I figure out my next moves."

"What about school?"

"I'm still going."

"That's good. You gotta keep going, Ryan. Don't screw yourself by not graduating."

"I won't. I promise you."

"Why'd you think I'd get mad?"

"Well, 'cuz I moved out about six months ago."

"And you've been going to school?"

"Yes!"

"I'd only be mad if you weren't going to school, so what's up?"

"Well, Mom said not to tell you 'cuz you'd stop paying her."

"She's right. I would've, and I would have given the money to you."

"You would?"

"Yeah. The money she gets is not for her; it's for you."

*

On a beautiful June afternoon, we explored the area where Ryan grew up. Driving around, we recognized some of the landmarks, sights, and areas he talked about. His graduation was a proud moment for Ryan and for us. Out on his own, he soldiered on and did it.

During dinner, we listened to him tell of his future plans. Afterward, my thoughts drifted back to my own feelings of accomplishment after graduating from high school and the excitement, hope, and wonder for what was ahead.

> *Consider it pure joy, my brothers and sisters,*
> *whenever you face trials of many kinds, because*

you know that the testing of your faith produces perseverance. Let perseverance finish its work so that you may be mature and complete, not lacking anything. If any of you lacks wisdom, you should ask God, who gives generously to all without finding fault, and it will be given to you. But when you ask, you must believe and not doubt, because the one who doubts is like a wave of the sea, blown and tossed by the wind. That person should not expect to receive anything from the Lord. Such a person is double-minded and unstable in all they do.[3]

14

The Getty[1] glowed majestic against the backdrop of the Santa Monica Mountains on a gorgeous morning, typical of Southern California that time of year. It was a postcard picture of infinite blue sky encircling an iconic scene that draws you into a life different from anywhere else.

"You okay?" Mike asked.

Turning from the window, my thoughts broke.

"Getting a migraine," I answered. "Was hoping to be in surgery by now. Think I can take any medicine?"

Surgery was scheduled for 9:00 a.m.; it was already 11:00.

Mike got up from his seat and walked out to the nurses' station.

Returning to the view outside, I took in the beauty. The mountains were dense and vibrantly green against the aura of the white structure. It was February 2015, and there had been some decent rain. It brought back memories of hiking with Todd. Picturing the views, I imagined being able to hike again with Mike and our dogs, maybe getting out and doing some camping.

But it was hard to enjoy anything while I was in so much pain. Even the view hurt with its reminder of what used to be.

Mike walked back in. "You can take a triptan."

We rode the elevator down to the parking lot in silence. Outside, it was still cool, not as crisp as a few hours ago when we first arrived.

The drive had been uneventful. Traffic was moderate until we hit I-10 where the second half of the 32-mile trip dragged on for a little over an hour. Living in Southern California had conditioned us to allow a lot of time to get anywhere.

We made our way to the car. As we walked, I realized I hadn't noticed the view on the way in. It wasn't as spectacular from ground level as it was from the fifth-story window. The quiet majesty of it also changed with the stinky odor and ominous buzz of the freeway. It was reminiscent of ants scurrying around their hill with the reek of dumpster in the air.

My mood was down. I needed change, but since I had injured my back, I felt trapped. I was hoping surgery would give me new life, a new perspective. With my head pounding, I rode the elevator back up with Mike, only to wait a couple more hours before finally being rolled into the preparation room.

*

Coming out of the anesthesia, I felt immense pain course through my back, and childhood terrors became fresh in my mind. Memories with so much detail had played out in a nightmare while I was on the operating table as if I were there again watching scenes before me as an adult out of my body.

"How are you feeling?" someone asked.

Pissed, my head screamed. What the . . . ? My tongue felt furry, but I managed to slur out the word *thirsty*, and then someone gave me ice chips to suck on.

With my eyes closed, I tried to ride out the DTs of the anesthesia wearing off. My head was still pounding, and my thoughts were spinning with events from earlier in my life as they tied themselves together with something that occurred later. By the time the nurse checked on me again, all I wanted to do was get up and run.

Then another voice: "We're taking you to your room now."

Mike walked in. Tears ran down my face and made everything hurt worse.

"Can I stand and walk to see how things feel?" I asked once the nurses had me situated.

I had no relief when I got up. I sucked in a deep breath, did a slow crawl around the room, and then laid back down. Recovery was going to be rough.

It was late in the afternoon by then, almost evening by the time Mike left. After we said goodbye, I tried to settle in and manage the pain level. The migraine had subsided but was making a comeback. Lying there staring at nothing, feeling abandoned and alone, I tried to push out the memories taunting me. But I was stuck in an ugly cycle, and the opiates were making it worse. Tears welled up in my eyes and then fell, snaking a path to my ears and flooding them.

"God, please. Why is the past coming back to haunt me, especially now?"

It was a half-hearted outreach to the Man I still hardly knew.

*

The next morning, I kept busy doing painfully slow laps around the hospital ward. I was bent over at about a 40-degree angle, gripping the guide rails along the walls and groaning with every step. It was the kind of groan you can't control. You want to, but the pain hits so sharply that it's instinctive and just leaks out.

Mike arrived with a big kiss and some real food.

"I missed you. The girls kept going to the door looking for you. Zeza even slept by the door." Our rescued Shepherd mix was my girl. It felt good to be missed.

An hour or so later, we made our way out of the hospital, a bag of pain meds and muscle relaxers in hand. The ride home was brutal. I laid down in the back seat, braced myself for any movement, and groaned uncontrollably the whole way.

As I got home and settled in, our dogs cuddled around me. Zeza was by my side. Sleep wouldn't come that night. The opiates had me wired, feeding the relentless ongoing migraine, so I stopped taking them. Unable to fend for myself the first week, Mike was my rock.

Like any couple, over the years we've shared with each other our upbringings and some of our hurts and hang-ups from past relationships. We've learned by trial and error, growth and respect. We are strengthened by our mutual desire to rise above the hell we were each raised in.

Even though I know of the violence and mayhem from Mike's upbringing, and vice versa, we've never gone into descriptive detail with each other, only surface descriptions like "I got my butt beat for that one!" I hadn't told him about the nightmare and how my emotions were extra raw.

While Mike helped me take a shower the first morning, I broke down in sobs.

"What's up?" he asked.

"This is so degrading."

"What? You wouldn't do the same for me?"

"Yes. You just don't get it. It sucks having to rely on someone, and you know how I am about my body."

Knowing he was looking at me, I wouldn't look at him. He's a much a better communicator, which can be annoying.

"Yeah, but I get to touch this." He teasingly ran the washcloth over my butt.

His grin broke me.

"Stop. You're not funny," I laughed through tears.

"You can't control everything. You have to let go and relax."

He was right. And it wasn't the first time I'd been told that, but not by him, which was what hit me. Those very same words had come to me several times after reaching out in prayer.

Not going into detail, I told Mike about the nightmare and how vivid it was. "It was like watching a movie but feeling the emotions of it at the same time because it was my experiences."

"Well, that's great. Just what you need to deal with now."

"But why?"

Neither of us had an answer.

*

It took a few days to get the opiates out of my system. Into the third week of recovery, the pain was subsiding but was still a lot. I kept trying to drown the memories with TV and e-games.

"Please, Lord. I need help," I cried out while stretched out on our living room recliner one day, hurting and fighting a migraine. It had been a while since I'd felt His presence.

After finishing the first season of *Bloodline* later that day, I flipped to the news. There was a reporter telling about a teen suicide—another one—in the Midwest. The rate was high that year, reportedly costing the United States approximately $69 billion.[2] I wept with the girl's parents as they spoke lovingly of her on TV, already advocating for prevention in their daughter's name.

I had always ignored the nudges to share about suicide and domestic violence. The nudge that day was a push. With my head throbbing, I turned off the TV, closed my eyes, and laid back. The rhythm of my pulse slowed and relaxed into the quiet, and I envisioned my happy place.

Several minutes went by, and I drifted back to reality.

"I want you to write" was softly impressed on my mind.

It took a minute to gain my composure.

"Okay. Could I get a little more direction, please?" I requested, looking up.

* * *

Physical therapy helped, but the pain was bad, and worry set in. Panic attacks hit. I was riding the roller coaster of anxiety and depression, and the past wouldn't be shoved back into the pit it crawled out of.

My prayers received no answers, and the silence hurt. The writing assignment was bugging me, but I was unsure of what exactly was being asked. I didn't feel ready, so I shoved it aside.

*

Back to work part time, I eased in to see how things felt. It was good to feel purposeful. In the work element, life seemed to move along again.

But everything was still all wrong. I was struggling, trying to keep going.

Sitting at my desk about six months after surgery, the nerve pain in my leg did a slow creep from my knee down into my foot. The pain was so much that after work, all I could manage was floating in the tub and then lying down. My social life declined. Mike and I struggled. Our intimacy took a hard hit.

Wanting to enjoy life and get back to it, I kept trudging along, hoping to find relief.

A pain management class was recommended. The latter half of the class was spent with a physical therapist to learn how pain works and try some mental exercises to help calm it.

A session or two in, Dr. Dell was teaching calming techniques.

"When you feel your pain level increasing, immediately stop what you're doing, rest, and work through it. Breathe. Find that place in your mind."

With our collective eyes closed, we were told to focus on the switch in our minds and "flip it off." Not finding the switch and only finding childhood pain and the things that caused it, I sobbed. Dr. Dell asked me to stay after class.

"You seem really distraught."

"I'm trying to keep going," I bawled and blubbered.

"Help me understand your pain. What's going on with you?"

"After the back injury, my pain gradually got worse over the years. Surgery didn't help, and now it's worse than ever."

"When your pain hits . . . "

"It's constant," I interrupted. "The level varies, but it's never even at a three for very long in the morning until it steadily increases."

"Let's try closing your eyes and calming your body and mind down."

She was a wonderful doctor and meant well. It wasn't just the pain; it was also the confusion of my place in life. Why was the past coming forward? What was I supposed to write? How do I talk about things of God? Was I hearing voices? Was I like Mom?

Not knowing what to say, I went with the first person who came to mind.

"When I close my eyes, all I see is my dad." It was kind of a spit, like it tasted bad.

"What about your dad?"

"He was violent, mean when he was around. He was brutal to my mom. I grew up lonely, but I've never really talked about it."

"You don't feel safe when you close your eyes?"

"I don't think I've ever felt safe."

"What's it going to take to make you feel safe?"

"Don't know."

"Would you like to speak with me regularly, one-on-one? Maybe get some of this out?"

There was something about Dr. Dell that made me want to open up, but I didn't know how to start talking about stuff from so long ago, and I felt stupid having to deal with it all these years later.

* * *

Deciding on an idea, I ran it past Sal, a colleague I had worked with and respected. Sal and I had shared some of our pasts in conversations over the years. Without much detail, he was aware I'd experienced domestic violence.

We knew each other as believers but had never discussed the depth of our conviction. Still a struggling Christian, I was afraid and unsure to tell Sal I'd been told to write after prayer one day. I didn't have an understanding of it myself.

"I've been thinking about writing a book about growing up in domestic violence. What do you think?"

Immediately, Sal scrunched up his face, one side of his mouth downturned. "I'm leery of people who do that. They're attention whores."

"Well, that's not the intent. It might help someone else going through crap."

"There are other ways of doing that without being a reality show," he shot back.

> It is better to take refuge in the LORD than to trust
> in humans.[3]

* * *

Confused but extremely curious, I had been pondering my faith and wanted to finally learn about and understand the Lord. But nobody I knew talked about things of the Bible.

Mike wasn't the one at that time. His viewpoint had taken a sour turn due to a heartbreaking fallout with his best friend, Jay. The woman that Jay had been dating for a while was a "Bible thumper," but her actions and attitude didn't follow suit. Jay went down a path that was destructive to many of his relationships.

Raised Catholic, Mike voiced negativity many times over the phoniness he perceived from that denomination. The child molestation and other crimes had made him bitter.

At the time, I was craving to really find God, while Mike seemed closed off.

The unspiritual self, just as it is by nature, can't receive the gifts of God's Spirit. There's no capacity for them. They seem like so much silliness. Spirit can be known only by spirit—God's Spirit and our spirits in open communion.[4]

* * *

I was enjoying the view of the San Gabriel Mountains out the window one day, with the palm trees in my line of sight swaying with the breeze and the sky an endless cool blue. There wasn't a cloud in sight.

"Lord, I really need to hear from You." With warm water pulsing from the showerhead kneading my back, my head was bowed.

Listening through the open window to the sounds of our neighborhood bustling about on a Saturday morning, I waited for a few minutes while some wild parrots sat in a tree, causing a ruckus. Then deflated and feeling directionless, I finished rinsing off.

Hoping the view would help my funk, I took another look out the window before turning off the water. The amazing expanse of sky was in front of me.

"Write the book." It was impressed on me just as softly as when He told me He wanted me to write.

It had been two years, and I broke into sobs. Avoiding it was just going further down the snake's hole. It was time to take heed.

I told Mike, "I'm thinking about writing a book about domestic violence. Everything going on lately has sparked something in me, and maybe speaking out could help someone."

"Go for it," he encouraged me.

* * *

My first session with Dr. Dell felt like a wreck. I was worse off going out than coming in.

"I thought I'd been going through life fine, that I'd gotten over things. But then during surgery . . . " I blubbered. I was angry and unsure of myself and everything about me, like when I was a kid with no idea how to deal with it.

"What do you use as an outlet?" Dr. Dell asked at one point.

"What do you mean?"

"How do you release what you're feeling? You said you don't talk about past stuff with anyone, and cramming it down doesn't work."

"Well, that's why I'm here with you now, I guess. I started writing recently."

"That's a terrific way for release. Keep going with it. Are you finding it therapeutic?"

"Not sure yet. Would you like to read some of it?"

"Absolutely."

*

The second session was worse.

"What happened?" Dr. Dell asked. "When you left last time, I thought you had relaxed some. You're so agitated today."

"It's the pain, Doc. Sitting is the worst. I can't keep going like this."

"We have to see if we can figure out why you're having so much pain. Do you think when you're agitated it's worse?"

"Of course. When the pain level hits a six and higher, calm goes out the window. My brain goes into panic mode."

"We need to find out what's going on with you. Is it okay if I refer you to our head of neurology to see if he can do something for you?"

"Please."

"I'll do that. You've mentioned a couple of times that you're someone who goes above and beyond, especially at work. Why?"

"Don't know. It's how I'm built."

"Do you think you overachieve for approval?"

That made me pause and hesitate to answer.

"Do you think the rejection you felt from your dad has driven you?"

I knew the answer, and I didn't want to say it, but I squeezed "yes" out of me. Then I added, "But I like to do a good job for people."

"Understood, but I want you to slow down. Let others pick up the slack."

"Doc, I'm not that way."

"Work on it."

Before leaving, I handed her an envelope. "Here's some of what I've written so far, as promised."

*

Mike and I took a long weekend away at our favorite oasis. It was a miserable trip. In a lot of pain, I broke down and disintegrated in front of Mike. In a heap on the floor, I told him I couldn't keep going. It wasn't the first time that death seemed better than living in chronic pain and not understanding my place.

*

The head of neuro, Dr. Ho, went over everything with me about my injury. Then he sat back in his chair.

"In my opinion, the nerve damage was already done before you had surgery. It was unnecessary and didn't help because the nerve issues had already gone on much longer than six months."

"So why was it even recommended? Why put me through all that?"

"Can't answer that. But there are options."

*

Our final visit came much sooner than expected. After we said our hellos, I shared with Dr. Dell.

"Doc, I've taken to heart how you told me to slow down and take care of myself. Mike and I have put a plan of action into place. It's going to take some time before the next steps with my back, so we're rolling with things changing and taking the opportunity to relocate."

"You deserve to get this all figured out. I wish you the best and love you."

"Thanks for all you've done for me. I'm going to miss you."

She stood up and gave me hug.

"Oh yeah, did you have a chance to read what I gave you?"

"I did! Please keep going with it. Share it."

* * *

Mike and I had confided in one another that we had been praying. It opened up a deep discussion of faith between us. We knew we had a long road ahead but felt on course and guided.

The move to Lake Havasu City, Arizona, happened fast. Within six weeks, we were packed up and gone.

*

"This was meant to be. God got us here," Mike said as we sat in the backyard, somewhat settled in.

"I've wanted to talk to you about something but have been afraid." I gave him a side-eye to see if he was ready.

"What's up?"

"I've been thinking about going back to church."

"Why would you be afraid to tell me that?"

"Because of what went on with you and Jay, the way you went off about it."

"That's a different situation. Do what you gotta do. I didn't mean to make you feel like that."

"There's something else."

"What's that?" He gave me the side-eye this time.

"Back when I told you about writing . . ." I paused, scared. ". . . it's because I was told to in response to prayer."

"Really," he cocked an eyebrow. "This should be interesting."

15

how the Lord you're serious. Just flip the switch on. It's a
dimmer switch, though. Once you turn the light on, you have
to work in cooperation with the Source to keep His strength
going, or the light goes dim in you.

Your word is a lamp for my feet, a light on my path.[1]

*By your words I can see where I'm going; they throw
a beam of light on my dark path.*[2]

With little idea where to begin, I prayed first.

"Okay, God." Sitting there for a while was discouraging because
nothing came. My mind went blank, so on went the TV. But the
light came through.

We had recently installed cable. As I flipped through the new
lineup, TBN popped up. TBN is a Christian channel, and Joyce
Meyer was teaching about not giving the devil a foothold. It hit
home, but it was confusing.

"Lord, I understand about things holding me back, but . . . "
Frustration hit.

The dogs and I headed outside into the warm Arizona sun and
looked out toward the Mohave Mountains.

"What bothers you the most?" He softly asked (not spoken, just impressed in my thoughts).

"The most? So much right now, Lord. Can I think on that?"

As I walked around the backyard talking to myself, doubt set in.

"The devil," Joyce Meyer said in my head, "will manipulate you . . ."

"God doesn't want me to doubt!" It was a shout and just shot out of me.

I froze in place to hear what was spoken next.

"What has bothered you the longest?"

It was really the first conversation, and it was strange—wonderfully strange.

"The curse!"

A volcano exploded in my brain as questions came pouring out.

"Why am I a sinner? I was just a little kid. I don't understand sin."

So I started at the beginning of the Bible. After a few chapters, I wanted to scream. The more I took in, the more questions I had—lots and lots of questions.

A cycle of anxiety and panic began as I questioned myself about what I was doing, my doubts about God, and what I was hearing from Him. My self-worth would take a hit.

> *This is no weekend war that we'll walk away from and forget about in a couple of hours. This is for keeps, a life-or-death fight to the finish against the Devil and all his angels. Be prepared. You're up against far more than you can handle on your own. Take all the help you can get, every weapon God has issued, so when it's all over but the shouting you'll still be on your feet. Truth, righteousness, peace, faith, and salvation are more than words. Learn how to apply them. You'll need them throughout your life. God's Word is an indispensable weapon.*[3]

In another translation of the Bible, this passage calls this the armor of God!

> *Finally, be strong in the Lord and in his mighty power. Put on the full armor of God, so that you can take your stand against the devil's schemes. For our struggle is not against flesh and blood, but against the rulers, against the authorities, against the powers of this dark world and against the spiritual forces of evil in the heavenly realms. Therefore put on the full armor of God, so that when the day of evil comes, you may be able to stand your ground, and after you have done everything, to stand. Stand firm then, with the belt of truth buckled around your waist, with the breastplate of righteousness in place, and with your feet fitted with the readiness that comes from the gospel of peace. In addition to all this, take up the shield of faith, with which you can extinguish all the flaming arrows of the evil one. Take the helmet of salvation and the sword of the Spirit, which is the word of God. And pray in the Spirit on all occasions with all kinds of prayers and requests. With this in mind, be alert and always keep on praying for all the Lord's people.*[4]

As my understanding grew, hunger for more urged me on. But the battle within me raged. Reaching out for help is one of the hardest things, but through the VA, I met Dr. Lumpkin. My first few sessions are a blur, a lot of tears and snot. During the first session, I mentioned wanting to get back to church. Doc shared that he's a Christian and encouraged me and suggested that I find a Bible study.

*

The first class was on hope. The teacher must have thought I was a nut because my eyes would tear up and open wide as we talked about who I am, who we all are, and what part of life this being human is all about.

As Jan taught, a particular verse struck me. "Full of hope, you'll relax, confident again; you'll look around, sit back, and take it easy."[5] It's what I wanted so very badly.

*

Digging my heels in, I searched for answers to some of the myths that plagued me, stuff we hear from others, on TV, and in the news as we live out our lives. They were things like God is angry and punishing; men wrote the Bible, it's not reliable; all the different translations have made the Bible a joke; the Bible isn't true; how did the Bible come about; the Bible's antiquated and says women are subservient; it condones rape and slavery; what does being born again really mean?

TBN helped show me the way.

I am grateful to Pastor Robert Morris for his three-part series: "How Do I Know There is a God? Jesus is the Only Way. The Bible is True."

Researching Bibles and finding a version with commentary I resonated with made me bug-eyed because understanding the spiritual world started seeping in, awakening me with more clarity.

> But don't fool yourselves. Don't let yourselves be poisoned by this anti-resurrection loose talk. "Bad company ruins good manners." Think straight. Awaken to the holiness of life. No more playing fast and loose with resurrection facts. Ignorance of God is a luxury you can't afford in times like these. Aren't you embarrassed that you've let this kind of thing go on as long as you have? Some skeptic is

sure to ask, "Show me how resurrection works. Give me a diagram; draw me a picture. What does this 'resurrection body' look like?" If you look at this question closely, you realize how absurd it is. There are no diagrams for this kind of thing. We do have a parallel experience in gardening. You plant a "dead" seed; soon there is a flourishing plant. There is no visual likeness between seed and plant. You could never guess what a tomato would look like by looking at a tomato seed. What we plant in the soil and what grows out of it don't look anything alike. The dead body that we bury in the ground and the resurrection body that comes from it will be dramatically different. You will notice that the variety of bodies is stunning. Just as there are different kinds of seeds, there are different kinds of bodies—humans, animals, birds, fish—each unprecedented in its form. You get a hint at the diversity of resurrection glory by looking at the diversity of bodies not only on earth but in the skies—sun, moon, stars—all these varieties of beauty and brightness. And we're only looking at pre-resurrection "seeds"—who can imagine what the resurrection "plants" will be like![6]

I dived back into Genesis with my new Bible, and it became my personal favorite—the book of beginnings and firsts. There's so much the Lord shows us in just the first four chapters. God pronounced all His creation good. Adam and Eve were the only two humans to know earth as the Lord God had intended it. God planted a special place for Himself in what He created—the Lord's Garden, Eden.[7] The Garden was His tabernacle, an amazing place of honor for the children of God to meet with Him. What an incredible scene to envision!

"We love Him because He first loved us."[8]

Picture your number-one getaway. It doesn't have to be a beautiful garden. It's the place where you feel most at peace. What makes it your favorite? Is it outdoors, or does it involve calm surroundings? Is it spiritual? Is it a blissful feeling you wish could last forever?

Adam and Eve lived like that and beyond. Our wildest imaginations can't fathom the perfect everything they were given.[9] Given. Just out of love by the Lord who created humans special, set apart, to have a relationship with Him.[10]

When we were set apart, the Lord gave us free will. He let us know from the beginning that we have choices.[11] God doesn't want robots. He also doesn't want us to feel forced but wants us to choose Him, to want to be with Him because we're family.

"But God demonstrates His own love toward us, in that while we were still sinners, Christ died for us."[12]

Jesus tells us to try. "Anyone who chooses to do the will of God will find out whether my teaching comes from God or whether I speak on my own."[13]

The Lord wants us to love Him as much as He loves us and revere Him as our Creator.

> And if it seems evil to you to serve the LORD, choose for yourselves this day whom you will serve, whether the gods which your fathers served that were on the other side of the River, or the gods of the Amorites, in whose land you dwell. But as for me and my house, we will serve the LORD.[14]

The only creation the Lord God directed Adam not to eat was the fruit of the Tree of the Knowledge of Good and Evil.[15] Everything else was Adam's, and when Eve came along, everything was theirs.

Enter the serpent, the most cunning of "any beast of the field which the LORD God had made."[16] This was not a serpent as we know it but something different that most likely had legs or walked upright since he was cursed by God to "crawl on your belly and you will eat dust all the days of your life."[17] But he wasn't just a serpent, as we learn later. He was Satan, formerly Lucifer.

The name *Lucifer* is translated from the Hebrew word *halal*, which means "brightness" or "morning star."[18] We're not told a lot about him, but we're told enough.

Ezekiel tells us about him. "You were the anointed cherub who covers; I established you; you were on the holy mountain of God; you walked back and forth in the midst of fiery stones."[19]

The Lord originally created Lucifer as an "anointed cherub!"

What's a cherub?[20] Basically, it's a winged angelic being that serves to guard and protect according to God's will, a symbol of God's authority whose primary role is to give glory, honor, and thanks to God.[21] After the fall, God protected humankind from an eternity of living in sin by banishing Adam and Eve from Eden before they could partake of the other important tree in the Garden, the Tree of Life. Then He protected the Garden with cherubim and a flaming sword.[22] Later, when Moses built the tabernacle, God told him that the veil made to protect the Holy of Holies was to have cherubim skillfully woven into it.[23]

Isaiah tells us of events before human history, the beginning of sin in the universe. He tells us of the fall of Satan for his pride, ego, and lust of self.

> *How you are fallen from heaven, O Lucifer, son of the morning! How you are cut down to the ground, you who weakened the nations! For you have said in your heart: "I will ascend into heaven, I will exalt my throne above the stars of God; I will also sit on the mount of the congregation on the farthest sides*

of the north; I will ascend above the heights of the clouds, I will be like the Most High." Yet you shall be brought down to Sheol, to the lowest depths of the Pit. Those who see you will gaze at you, And consider you, saying: "Is this the man who made the earth tremble, who shook kingdoms, who made the world as a wilderness and destroyed its cities, who did not open the house of his prisoners?[24]

Jesus himself told 72 disciples, "I saw Satan fall like lightning from heaven."[25] Was this when hell was created for the devil and his angels?

Satan took a third of the angels with him. Just like Adam and Eve, they rejected the perfect environment that God created for them.

"His tail drew a third of the stars of heaven and threw them to the earth. And the dragon stood before the woman who was ready to give birth, to devour her Child as soon as it was born."[26]

"Then he will say to those on his left, 'Depart from me, you who are cursed, into the eternal fire prepared for the devil and his angels.'"[27]

Hell wasn't even created for us! But it had to enlarge itself because of our sin!

*Therefore Sheol has enlarged itself
And opened its mouth beyond measure;
Their glory and their multitude and their pomp,
And he who is jubilant, shall descend into it.
People shall be brought down,
Each man shall be humbled,
And the eyes of the lofty shall be humbled.*[28]

So Satan took control of the serpent.[29] Adam and Eve lived with the animals in close relation it seems because Eve wasn't surprised that he was talking. Using the serpent's God-given gifts, Satan approached Eve to change the course of humankind.

Why?

The word *Satan* is the English translation of a Hebrew word for "adversary."[30] Many times in the Bible, God renamed people to establish a new identity according to His purpose.[31]

Satan opposed God in heaven, went from being God's "morning star" to His "adversary," and then he was banished to earth.

Still God's adversary on earth, he tempted Eve.[32] First, he lowered God's authority in the conversation by removing His Lordship. When Eve responded, she either embellished what Adam had relayed to her or Adam did because the Lord God didn't tell Adam that "neither shall you touch it."[33]

The serpent probably saw another opening and cut deep, contradicting the Lord by telling Eve she wouldn't die but that her eyes would be opened and she would "be like God."[34]

Lust hit Eve when she saw that "the tree was good for food," "it was pleasant to the eyes," and "desirable to make one wise."[35] She caved to temptation and sinned by going against the Lord God's command. Then she gave some to Adam, "and he ate."[36]

Adam failed to protect the perfect kingdom God had made him responsible for and allowed sin to enter.[37] What if he had corrected Eve? It doesn't matter; God knew what was going to happen.[38]

Did the serpent transform before their eyes when it was cursed?

What must Satan have thought? That he'd succeeded? That God would now destroy humankind?

Did the consequences of Adam and Eve's sin really hit them?[39] We know their eyes were opened and they knew nakedness, so shame set in. Or was it going to take some more living for it to really sink in?

It doesn't matter. Sin had entered earth.

It should have been their deaths, but God performed the first sacrifices to atone for their sins and cover their naked bodies. It must have been horrifying for Adam and Eve to experience the

death of animals, especially because of something they had done—
more guilt.

And it was a wake-up call to Satan that the Lord had a redemption
plan. Now Satan had to find the right seed.

Adam was cursed to labor and work for the food God had free-
ly supplied to Eve and him. The land was no longer Paradise; it was
cursed. Now there would be "thorns and thistles."[40]

Sexual relations came about. Eve's first pregnancy was a son,
Cain. All those incredible firsts! Then they had another son, Cain's
brother, Abel.[41] Were they a happy family? Up until . . .

Over the course of time, most likely when the boys reached
the appropriate age, Cain and Abel brought the Lord offerings of
firstfruits.[42] God accepted Abel's offering but not Cain's. Only God
knows our hearts.

"A person may think their own ways are right, but the LORD
weighs the heart."[43]

From another translation, this verse says, "We justify our actions by appearances; God examines our motives."[44]

Cain got angry at God and jealous of Abel. As any father would
do, God corrected Cain and gave him a warning, a choice. But Cain
did his own thing and killed his brother.[45]

It was the rolling chain reaction of eating the forbidden
fruit.[46]

*

During another chat with Dr. Lumpkin, he told me about Life
Groups at the church he attends. A class on Priscilla Shirer's book
Discerning the Voice of God opened up a whole new dimension of
the world to me.

Scared to death walking into a women's group, I almost turned
around, but a petite, bubbly blond came up to me with the warmest
greeting.

"Hi, I'm Elaine. Welcome. Are you new to Calvary?"

So nervous, I wanted to puke but managed to introduce myself and shake Elaine's hand with my sweaty one. She made me a name tag and then ushered me into a classroom.

*

Aside from boot camp, weddings, and funerals, it was the first group prayer experience since leaving the church 38 years before.

Tears flowed during every class. I was embarrassed at first, but the overwhelming feeling of safety kept me going back. God took me baby step by baby step.

"You're here for Me," He let me know as I voiced my fears through prayer.

*

One of the first exercises we had to do was identify the reasons we don't obey the Lord. My top two were fear and concern I might be hearing Him wrong. After a few more lessons, I discovered there were many more reasons I didn't obey the Lord, and those discoveries shook me. I had a pride issue of "flying solo." Literally, it was a motto of mine. Other reasons included a lack of trust in God, impatience with His timing, feeling unworthy, and doubt, to name a few.

The second week, we studied the Holy Spirit, someone I knew very little about. It was another awakening.

Papa Joe had opened my eyes to Jesus, but the flood that hit when I studied the Holy Spirit and how He came to us helped bring things into perspective.

"Anyone can have a whole and lasting life"[47] because God sent His Son through spiritual seed to be born a human, to go through everything and more than we ever will because Jesus died with the weight of the sins of every human—all of us, past, present, and future.

The blood ran from Christ's wounds—His hands for the hands that ate the forbidden fruit; His feet to fulfill prophecy; His side where Eve was created; His head from the thorns and thistles of the curse assigned to Adam, now worn as a cruel crown on our Savior.

Even though God sent His Son,[48] Jesus volunteered![49]

> *This righteousness is given through faith in Jesus Christ to all who believe. There is no difference between Jew and Gentile, for all have sinned and fall short of the glory of God, and all are justified freely by his grace through the redemption that came by Christ Jesus. God presented Christ as a sacrifice of atonement, through the shedding of his blood—to be received by faith. He did this to demonstrate his righteousness, because in his forbearance he had left the sins committed beforehand unpunished—he did it to demonstrate his righteousness at the present time, so as to be just and the one who justifies those who have faith in Jesus.*[50]

And because of what Jesus did for us, God tells us, "They'll get to know me by being kindly forgiven, with the slate of their sins forever wiped clean."[51]

When it really hit me that my sins are forgiven, a warm flood of relief flowed through to my inner core and awakened my soul. I felt a new meaning of freedom as the weight of mistakes and wrongs were lifted. It changed me and made me start singing praises to God when I didn't even know the words, forgiving people and loving on others just because I felt and knew the love of the Father. Suddenly, everything had a purpose—past, present, and future.

"Create in me a pure heart, O God, and renew a steadfast spirit within me."[52]

God the Father. God the Son. God the Holy Spirit.

Jesus tells us straight up, "I and the Father are one."[53]

In John, chapter 14, the Apostle John shares that Jesus's disciples were confused about where He was telling them He was going and why.

Jesus told them, "I am the way and the truth and the life. No one comes to the Father except through me. If you really know me, you will know my Father as well. From now on, you do know him and have seen him."[54]

Here is my take. If you know Jesus, you know His Father. Jesus is His Father. Jesus is God, God the Son. You can't know the Father without knowing His Son. Jesus is the way, the truth, and the life through the Father.

John goes on to tell us that Philip asked of Jesus, "show us the Father and that will be enough for us."[55]

Jesus answered: "Don't you know me, Philip, even after I have been among you such a long time? Anyone who has seen me has seen the Father. How can you say, 'Show us the Father'? Don't you believe that I am in the Father, and that the Father is in me? The words I say to you I do not speak on my own authority. Rather, it is the Father, living in me, who is doing his work. Believe me when I say that I am in the Father and the Father is in me; or at least believe on the evidence of the works themselves."[56]

Then Jesus told them about the Holy Spirit.

If you love me, keep my commands. And I will ask the Father, and he will give you another advocate to help you and be with you forever—the Spirit of truth. The world cannot accept him, because it neither sees him nor knows him. But you know him, for he lives

with you and will be in you. I will not leave you as
orphans; I will come to you. Before long, the world
will not see me anymore, but you will see me. Because
I live, you also will live. On that day you will realize
that I am in my Father, and you are in me, and I am
in you. Whoever has my commands and keeps them
is the one who loves me. The one who loves me will
be loved by my Father, and I too will love them and
show myself to them.[57]

Later, in Chapter 20, John tells us about Jesus's resurrection. When Jesus meets up with His disciples again in His renewed, heavenly body, He lets them know He has just come from the Father and that His promised Helper was on the way.[58]

Thomas wasn't with the disciples at that time, though. Eight days later, they all met up with Thomas in attendance. Jesus joined them again by somehow entering the locked room. He cured Thomas's doubts.[59]

What Jesus says next is one of my favorite verses of faith. "Because you have seen me, you have believed; blessed are those who have not seen and yet have believed."[60]

*

The ancients of the Old Testament knew nothing of what we know. For them, God grew their faith by manifesting Himself in all kinds of ways.[61] He spoke many times—from the beginning.[62] He spoke as a theophany[63] when wrestling with Jacob.[64] Daniel tells about the hand mysteriously appearing and writing on the wall.[65] There are so many.

My personal favorite is the Battle of Jericho.[66] The Lord got crazy with that test of faith. Can you imagine the participants? Sorry, the Lord wants us to . . . do what? All right, we'll give it a shot. Then it worked, and the walls came down.

New Testament ancients passed down their stories on scrolls.[67] Then there was the physical and resurrected Jesus, and finally the Holy Spirit.[68]

The Word of God was given to us through the ancient scrolls and writings. Peter made sure to let us know that God's Word comes from God.[69] "All Scripture is God-breathed and is useful for teaching, rebuking, correcting and training in righteousness, so that the servant of God may be thoroughly equipped for every good work."[70]

When we accept Jesus into our lives, the Holy Spirit enters us. Paul, speaking about Jesus, teaches us in Ephesians, "And you also were included in Christ when you heard the message of truth, the gospel of your salvation. When you believed, you were marked in him with a seal, the promised Holy Spirit, who is a deposit guaranteeing our inheritance until the redemption of those who are God's possession—to the praise of his glory."[71]

When it sinks into your mind and soul that the same power that raised Jesus from the grave is within you, within us, it's like sucking in a deep, clean breath of fresh mountain air after exiting the gas chamber.

"And if the Spirit of him who raised Jesus from the dead is living in you, he who raised Christ from the dead will also give life to your mortal bodies because of his Spirit who lives in you."[72]

"For we were all baptized by one Spirit so as to form one body—whether Jews or Gentiles, slave or free—and we were all given the one Spirit to drink."[73]

Jesus explained to His disciples, to us, the access the Spirit gives.

> *I have much more to say to you, more than you can now bear. But when he, the Spirit of truth, comes, he will guide you into all the truth. He will not speak on his own; he will speak only what he hears, and he will tell you what is yet to come. He will glorify me because it is from me that he will receive what he will*

make known to you. All that belongs to the Father is mine. That is why I said the Spirit will receive from me what he will make known to you.[74]

Every pore in my body awakened as if freshly swiped by a cooling alcohol pad. It was as if the Spirit moved through me to tell me that my hand had been on the key the entire time but had just never completed the turn to unlock the door and release the family curse. It was gone, and I understood that. Christ was my Savior and had been in me the whole time. *Joy* isn't a word I normally use, but finally I knew joy.

That is the experience, the enlightenment of the Holy Spirit from the blood of Jesus, when you know you're on your way Home.

* * *

It was time to move forward and attend church. The service was on a Saturday evening, and a battle raged within me the entire day. Every time the words "What are you . . ." started in my thinking, I shouted, "Shut up! God doesn't want me to doubt. I can do all things through Christ Jesus."[75] I watched every hour go by.

Getting ready to go, thoughts of walking up the hill to church with Todd the first time went through the theater of my mind, playing over and over, and an overwhelming sadness hit. Loneliness.

"Here you are. All by yourself," my mind teased.

Dropping my hairbrush, I walked outside to look out over the lake at the Chemehuevi Mountains. I wasn't alone. All the players were there. It was like a courtroom in my head.

The accuser: "Here she is. Look at her."

Me: "You're not ready for this."

My Mediator: "She is ready. All she needs are her keys. She's not alone."

I cast that bad spirit into the lake, shooed the dogs back inside, and headed out.

With my car radio playing loudly, my thoughts were distracted. While I was parking, a wave of anxiety hit. I rested my head on the steering wheel. "Lord, please . . . "

"I am here," He impressed.

Walking in, I thought my knees would buckle. But God's incredible being was present. Sitting as remotely as possible, I knew it was going to be an emotional experience.

My tears flowed as we worshipped. It was the first time I had heard the song "Tremble" by Mosaic MSC, and it was powerful.

Making it back to church that day was worth every battle.

*

Bible study was like a therapy session. As others shared their experiences, pain, and losses, my tears ran as I held in my own pain. It took until about the third or fourth week to allow my voice to speak over my emotions. Opening up was freeing. A spectacular group of ladies took me under their collective spiritual wings and helped guide my way.

As my prayer life progressed, so did communication with the Lord. Going "boldly to the throne of grace,"[76] I asked for healing in my health. The chronic pain and migraines continued relentlessly, and health care was agonizingly slow. As a group, the women had prayed over situations for one another several times, and I witnessed the power of their prayers.

Within a couple of weeks, I discovered that most of my migraines were likely caused by degenerated discs in my neck, and the outlook was positive.

* * *

By the end of the seven-week Bible study, I felt like a hot mess all over again. I couldn't figure it out and then realized I was trying too hard. I took it to prayer.

"Keep going," the Spirit urged.

When the next study started, I felt like I was plodding through goo to get to the first few classes, and I couldn't leave fast enough when they were over.

It was the same with church. I was so sick of crying. Calvary felt right, but I didn't.

My next prayer went something like this: "Lord, You're everything, our Creator, our Father. You are our Master Counselor in heaven. Please, what is it? Show me how to release these tears. I'm over it!" It happened at church during communion. The music started, but I waited to stand and sat there, head bowed, until I heard back.

"You can let her go now."

"Who?" It was a quick thought question back and sounded sort of rude. "Sorry. Who, Lord?"

"You."

"What?"

I pondered that for days. I can let me go now? So I asked God one morning, "Father, do You mean die to self? I thought that's what I'm attempting to do, but now I'm not sure."

"Child, let *her* go." The word *her* was emphasized.

But "child" hit me.

I took it to Dr. Lumpkin.

"I think God's telling me to let the little girl in me go. Crying in church is what I did. It was my safe place. But it isn't the same experience anymore. It doesn't have to be like that."

"It sounds like you're still battling spiritually," Doc responded. "It's said that the harder you battle, the harder they fight back."

That's cringe-worthy!

"In your subconscious, that's where those memories are. Talk to them. Bring them forward, and tell her she's safe. Show her."

It's a process, but it works. Through prayer, reaching back to my younger self with the Lord, my tears gradually subsided.

*

Mike had been along for the ride the entire time.

"You scope it out," he had told me. "When you're comfortable at church, then . . . "

He still needed time. After attending church by myself for about six months, I hit him up.

"If you're off work early enough, want to go to church with me?"

An eyebrow went up, but then he smiled and said, "Yes."

It was an unforgettable experience to feel God's presence around me at different times, now knowing Him and being there with Mike. It was cosmic, like we were one with God. What the Word teaches about marriage hit me like a flood. Praising the Lord that day, we were two people, husband and wife, with God—a triune unit. As the lights danced with the music in church, it felt as if we were a prism and could jump on a beam into the light and touch Home.

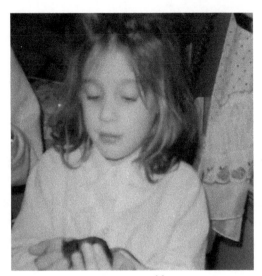

Five years old

The ring and necklace Mom made

Tom and I, ages five and ten

Dad with Tom and me

Mom when she got home after Todd was born

The four of us a couple of years later

Child's grave marker

Baba

Dad and Aunt Mitza

Zebbie

My room

Lil's house

The Three Musketeers together again after our long separation

a publication for outstanding high school art and literature

VI No. 3   THE POST-JOURNAL, Jamestown, New York—Monday, November 29, 1982   ©The Ogden Newspapers, Inc.   SEVEN

Rainbows of the Heart

Rainbows are like
The loves of the heart,
One sunny day a
Love may appear,
But like a rainbow
it soon fades away
As a lost pigment of
A wonderless imagination.

Traci
Jamestown

The United Methodist Church

Certificate of
Confirmation and Reception

This Certifies That

Traci

was confirmed as a member of Christ's holy
Church and received into the membership of the

_____**Kidder Memorial**_____
Church
at _____**Jamestown, N.Y.**_____
on _____**March 30**_____, 19 **80**

Pastor

222

Reverend Modisher being a goofball while in Kentucky with his wife looking on

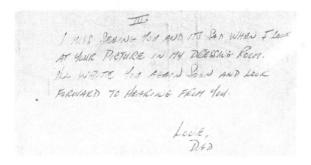

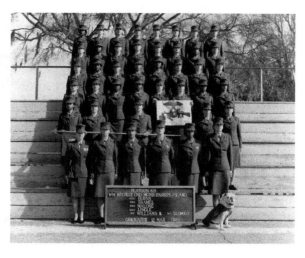

A stop home before California. Jimmy, Lil, Todd, and Dad

Tasha and her kittens

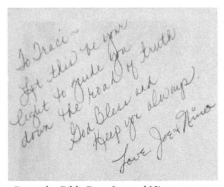

From the Bible Papa Joe and Nina gave me

Ryan, three years old

NOTES

Introduction

1. Domestic Violence. *Merriam-Webster.* https://www.merriam-webster.com/dictionary/domestic%20violence.
2. Eph. 2:10
3. Rom. 15:4–5 MSG
4. Ps.139 MSG
5. Gen. 34
6. Judges 19–21
7. 2 Sam. 13
8. Gal. 3:28 ESV
9. Rom. 12:19
10. Sherry Hamby et al., "Children's Exposure to Intimate Partner Violence and Other Family Violence," *Juvenile Justice Bulletin,* October 2011, https://www.ncjrs.gov/pdffiles1/ojjdp/232272.pdf.
11. Heb. 9:27–28 MSG

Chapter 1

1. *The Wizard of Oz,* directed by Victor Fleming (1939; Warner Bros.), https://www.warnerbros.com/movies/wizard-oz/.
2. "Willoughby, Ohio," *Ohio History Central,* http://www.ohiohistorycentral.org/w/Willoughby,_Ohio.
3. "Serbian Ohioans," *Ohio History Central,* http://www.ohiohistorycentral.org/w/Serbian_Ohioans.

Chapter 2

1. "Tom & Jerry," *Warner Bros.,* https://www.wbkidsgo.com/tom-and-jerry.
2. "The Pearl City," *City of Jamestown,* http://www.jamestownny.net/community-history/the-pearl-city/.
3. "Welcome to 59 Lucy Lane, Celoron, NY!" *LucyLane.com,* https://www.59lucylane.com/.

Chapter 3

1. *Bill & Ted's Excellent Online Adventure,* http://www.billandted.org/.
2. "Muttley," *Hanna-Barbera,* https://hanna-barbera.fandom.com/wiki/Muttley.
3. *The Twilight Zone,* IMDb, https://www.imdb.com/title/tt0052520/.
4. Manfred Mann's Earth Band, https://www.manfredmann.co.uk/.

Chapter 5

1. Exod. 3:14 NKJV
2. John 8:58
3. "Yahweh," *Britannica,* https://www.britannica.com/topic/Yahweh.

Chapter 6

1. Exod. 34:7
2. Gen. 9:12–16
3. Heb. 4:12 MSG
4. Gen. 1:27
5. Gen. 6:9–7:9
6. 1 Kings 17:4–6
7. Matt. 10:29 NKJV
8. Num. 22:22–34 NKJV
9. Ps. 104 MSG
10. Job 38–41 NKJV
11. Ps. 119:18

Chapter 8

1. "Identification Friend or Foe," *Raytheon*, https://www.raytheon.com/uk/capabilities/products/identification-friend-or-foe.
2. Ps. 139:7–12

Chapter 9

1. Rom. 8:5–8
2. Prov. 3:5–6 ESV

Chapter 10

1. 2 Sam. 11–12 ESV
2. Ps. 139:13–16 ESV
3. 2 Sam. 12:21–23 ESV
4. Isa. 41:10

Chapter 11

1. Ps. 32:8
2. Rom. 8:1
3. Matt. 6:14–15
4. Ps. 103:9–14

Chapter 12

1. Ps. 34:4–6 MSG
2. 1 John 1:8–10 MSG
3. James 5:16–20 MSG
4. Prov. 27:17 MSG
5. Eccles. 4:9–12 MSG
6. "Legend of the Dreamcatcher," *Native American Vault*, https://www.nativeamericanvault.com/pages/legend-of-the-dreamcatcher.
7. Exod. 20:3–6 MSG
8. 1 Cor. 10:14

Chapter 13
1. Matt. 15:8
2. "What Is Bonsai?" *Bonsai Empire*, https://www.bonsaiempire. com/origin.
3. James 1:2–8

Chapter 14
1. "The Getty Center," *Getty*, http://www.getty.edu/visit/center/.
2. "Learn the Latest Statistics on Suicide," *American Foundation for Suicide Prevention*, https://afsp.org/about-suicide/suicide-statistics/.
3. Ps. 118:8
4. 1 Cor. 2:14 MSG

Chapter 15
1. Ps. 119:105
2. Ps. 119:105 MSG
3. Eph. 6:12–17 MSG
4. Eph. 6:10–18
5. Job 11:18 MSG
6. 1 Cor. 15:33–41 MSG
7. Gen. 1:31–2:8 NKJV
8. 1 John 4:19 NKJV
9. Isa. 55:8–9
10. Ps. 4:3 NKJV
11. Gen. 2:16–17 NKJV
12. Rom. 5:8 NKJV
13. John 7:17
14. Josh. 24:15 NKJV
15. Gen. 2:7–9, 15–17 NKJV
16. Gen. 3:1 NKJV
17. Gen. 3:14

18. "Lucifer," *Strong's Exhaustive Concordance*, on Bible Hub, http://biblehub.net/searchhebrew.php?q=lucifer.
19. Ezek. 28:14 NKJV
20. "Cherubim," *Bible Study Tools*, https://www.biblestudytools.com/dictionary/cherubim-1/.
21. Rev. 4:8–9 NKJV
22. Gen. 3:22–24
23. Exod. 26:31–35
24. Isa. 14:12–17 NKJV
25. Luke 10:18 NKJV
26. Rev. 12:4 NKJV
27. Matt. 25:41
28. Isa. 5:14–15 NKJV
29. Rev. 12:9 NKJV
30. "Satan," *Strong's Concordance*, on Bible Hub, https://biblehub.com/str/hebrew/7854.htm.
31. Gen. 17:5, 15; 32:28 NKJV
32. Gen. 3:1–7 NKJV
33. Gen. 3:3
34. Gen. 3:4–5
35. Gen. 3:6 NKJV
36. Gen. 3:6 NKJV
37. Gen. 1:26–27
38. Rom. 11:34–36 MSG
39. Gen. 3:8–19 NKJV
40. Gen. 3:17–19 NKJV
41. Gen. 4:1–2 NKJV
42. Gen. 4:3–5 NKJV
43. Prov. 21:2
44. Prov. 21:2 MSG
45. Gen. 4:6–8
46. Rom. 5:12 MSG

47. John 3:16 MSG
48. Gal. 4:4–5 NKJV
49. John 10:14–18
50. Rom. 3:22–26
51. Heb. 8:12 MSG
52. Ps. 51:10
53. John 10:30
54. John 14:6–7
55. John 14:8
56. John 14:9–11
57. John 14:15–21
58. John 20:19–23
59. John 20:24–28
60. John 20:29
61. Heb. 1:1–2
62. Gen. 1:3
63. "What Is an Epiphany?" *Got Questions*, https://www.gotquestions.org/epiphany.html.
64. Gen. 32:22–32
65. Dan. 5:5
66. Josh. 6
67. Luke 4:17
68. Acts 2:1–13
69. 2 Pet. 1:19–21 ESV
70. 2 Tim. 3:16–17
71. Eph. 1:13–14
72. Rom. 8:11
73. 1 Cor. 12:13
74. John 16:12–15
75. Phil. 4:13
76. Heb. 4:16 NKJV

CPSIA information can be obtained
at www.ICGtesting.com
Printed in the USA
BVHW051354150721
612047BV00012B/422